Caring for youth in shelters

Effective strategies for professional caregivers

Also from the Boys Town Press

Books
Teaching Social Skills to Youth
Basic Social Skills
Treating Youth with DSM-IV Disorders: The Role of Social Skill Instruction
Dangerous Kids
Skills for Families, Skills for Life
Safe and Effective Secondary Schools
The Well-Managed Classroom
The Well-Managed Classroom for Catholic Schools
Getting Along With Others: Activity Book
Common Sense Parenting (also in Spanish)
Unmasking Sexual Con Games: Helping Teens Identify Good and Bad Relationships
Working With Aggressive Youth
The Ongoing Journey: Awakening Spiritual Life in At-Risk Youth
Building Skills in High-Risk Families: Strategies for the Home-Based Practitioner
Rebuilding Children's Lives: A Blueprint for Treatment Foster Parents
Effective Skills for Child-Care Workers
What Makes Boys Town Successful
A Good Friend: How to Make One, How to Be One
Who's in the Mirror? Finding the Real Me
What's Right for Me? Making Good Choices in Relationships
Boundaries: A Guide for Teens

Audio/Videotapes
Common Sense Parenting: Helping Your Child Succeed
Common Sense Parenting: Teaching Responsible Behavior
Videos for Parents Series
Sign With Me: A Family Sign Language Curriculum Series
Read With Me: Storytelling with Deaf Toddlers
One to One: Personal Listening Tapes for Teens
Common Sense Parenting Audiobook

For a free copy of the Boys Town Press catalog, call **1-800-282-6657**.
Or see us at our WEB site: www.girlsandboystown.org/btpress

Parents or children in trouble or having problems can call the
Boys Town National Hotline anytime, toll-free, at **1-800-448-3000**.

63-004
9910-19-0008

Caring for youth in shelters

Effective strategies for professional caregivers

▶ **by Roger W. Peterson, M.H.D.,
Gina A. Baker, M.H.D.,
Marcus A. Weiseth, B.A.**

BOYS TOWN PRESS

BOYS TOWN, NEBRASKA

The Boys Town Press is the publishing
division of Girls and Boys Town, the
original Father Flanagan's Boys' Home.

Caring for youth in shelters

Published by The Boys Town Press
Father Flanagan's Boys' Home
Boys Town, Nebraska 68010

ISBN 0-938510-99-1

10   9   8   7   6   5

Acknowledgments

This book would not have been possible without the generous work of many helping hands along the way. Boys Town Emergency Shelter Services wishes to offer a huge thanks to all Boys Town staff, past and present, who have contributed to the development of the ideas we share on the following pages. Their personal contributions have laid the foundation for the Boys Town Emergency Shelter Services program.

A special thanks goes to all the children and families who have participated in our shelter programs over the years; to Youth Care Workers in Boys Town Shelters who strive each day to bring troubled, needy children and their families back together; to the staff of the Boys Town Press for their editing and encouragement; to the staff of all Family-Based Programs; and especially to Gina and Dave Baker of the Boys Town Mid-Plains Shelter and the staff of the Boys Town Emergency Shelter Services program.

Table of contents

Introduction

When Father Edward Flanagan took in five homeless boys off the streets of Omaha, Nebraska, in 1917, he started a revolution that would forever change the way this country cares for its children. With love and compassion, Father Flanagan created Boys Town, a home for homeless and troubled children who had nowhere else to turn.

Since that time, Father Flanagan's ideas and ideals have lived on at Boys Town. Boys Town's Home Campus programs have touched the lives of thousands of boys and girls who needed someone to care about them. Many more young people and families have received help through programs that grew out of the original Boys Town concept.

Change has been constant at Boys Town through the decades. As the problems of youth became more complex and more compelling, new ways to deal with them were identified and fulfilled. At the same time, the basic goals of Boys Town – to instill in youngsters the values of love of God, respect for self and others, hard work, and a good education – remained unchanged.

Today, Boys Town is reaching out to troubled youth in ways Father Flanagan could only dream of. Under the leadership of Father Val J. Peter, the Boys Town Family Home Program has stretched across the nation, and other programs have been developed to offer help to children, parents, families, and other child-care organizations. The following programs have led the way in Boys Town's effort to care for more young people.

- **The Family Home Program** is the source of all Boys Town training and technology, and the foundation of almost every other Boys

Town program. This program is based at the Home Campus, where more than 550 boys and girls live in 75 family-style homes that make up the Village of Boys Town.

- **Boys Town USA** is responsible for the expansion of Boys Town's programs and development of Family Home sites in other states.

- **The Boys Town National Resource and Training Center** provides training and technical assistance to Boys Town USA Sites and to child-care organizations around the country. Training and technical assistance is available in these areas: shelter care, parent training, family preservation, treatment foster care, residential group home, education, residential treatment, and specialized workshops.

- **The Boys Town National Hotline**, which receives more than 1,000 calls a day, provides assistance to young people and adults across the country. Callers can dial the Hotline's toll free number (1-800-448-3000) to talk about such problems as physical and sexual abuse, alcoholism, drug abuse, suicide, and running away.

Providing emergency shelter care for youth is an integral part of Boys Town's mission. This manual is designed to teach Youth Care Workers their roles and duties as they help care for troubled children in youth shelters, and help bring these children and their families back together. The content is based on the technology developed and used by Boys Town Emergency Shelter Services, but the information can easily be adapted by other shelter programs (staff-secure detention facilities, short-term residential crisis centers,

etc.). In addition to presenting the technical aspects of the Boys Town program, many examples of how program components can be used on the job are included.

Shelter administrators also can use this manual as a guide for carrying out their mission of providing help for youth and their families in and beyond the shelter environment.

We welcome your decision to join us in our mission to help young people. We hope that providing you with the knowledge and proven methods you'll need to effectively care for youth, either as a Youth Care Worker in a Boys Town Shelter or in an outside program, will help you fulfill your role in that mission.

The following section includes a brief description of the Boys Town Emergency Shelter Services program.

Emergency Shelter Services program

Boys Town's Emergency Shelter Services program began serving children and families in March of 1989 with the opening of the Mid-Plains Shelter in central Nebraska, near Grand Island. Since then, Boys Town Shelters have opened in eight metropolitan areas from the East Coast to the West Coast.

A Boys Town Shelter, regardless of where it is located, can provide services for about 250 to 350 children each year. The exact number of children served depends on how long they stay, and on existing contracts with state and federal authorities.

Boys Town Shelters take in children who are between the ages of 10 and 18. The average length of stay is two to four weeks.

A Boys Town Shelter usually is staffed by several full-time Youth Care Workers, a Shelter Coordinator, a Shelter Supervisor, a Family Interventionist, and a secretary. Some shelters have Common Sense Parenting or Family Preservation staff members, who help provide a comprehensive treatment approach. Volunteers also work with children and families who seek help through shelter programs. All work together to provide children with a safe place to stay and to bring families back together.

Some children come to Boys Town Shelters on their own. Some are brought in by their families. Others are referred by a variety of sources: probation offices, the courts, social services departments, caseworkers, and mental health professionals.

Children who enter a shelter may be in trouble with the law or at school, or are experiencing difficulties in their family life. They may have been thrown out of their homes, or abused or neglected by their parents or other adults.

Boys Town Shelters will accept almost all children, except those who are a danger to themselves or others. The Shelter Coordinator makes the final decision on admissions, and follows the policies and procedures that ensure the safety of all the children who receive treatment at the shelter.

The shelters are set up to allow staff to easily monitor the children and provide a safe treatment environment. Bedrooms for girls are located in a different wing or on a different floor than the boys' bedrooms. There are game rooms and private rooms where children can meet with families, counselors, caseworkers, probation officers, etc.

As a Youth Care Worker, you must be well-prepared for the responsibilities and duties required in any shelter program. It is a stressful, demanding profession, and effective training and program knowledge are necessities.

As we have served troubled children and families in different areas of the country, we have come to realize that there is a lot more to shelter care than simply feeding, clothing, and giving children a place to stay for a while. Therefore, we use the same treatment technology as the Boys Town Family Home Program, adapted to a much shorter time frame. And, we provide many other services, including mediation, follow-up, and aftercare, which help us reach beyond the shelter to youth and families in need.

As you read this manual, keep in mind your mission and goal – making a difference by helping the children and families who will come to you when they have no place left to turn.

CHAPTER ONE

Professionalism

Bill, a Boys Town Youth Care Worker, has just spent the last 45 minutes dealing with an out-of-control child. The youth has calmed down and is practicing a new skill with Bill. The phone rings, and an angry parent shouts his displeasure about the shelter "not helping my kid." Bill doesn't shout back or hang up. Instead, he says, "I understand that you are concerned about your child. I would be glad to talk about it. Thanks for lowering your voice." Bill is a professional.

As with any profession, you, as a Youth Care Worker in a shelter program, must meet certain expectations and assume certain responsibilities in order to do your job well and represent your program in a favorable manner.

Professionalism in the Boys Town Emergency Shelter Services program is defined by these nine basic areas of behavior, that can be used as guidelines by any shelter program.

1. Conscientious implementation of the program

2. Appropriate modeling

3. Communication and general social skills

4. Confidentiality

5. Contact with supervisor

6. Positive consumer relationships

7. Respecting cultural diversity

8. Continued development of professional skills

9. Giving and receiving feedback

Improving the skills associated with these areas promotes professional growth, enhances your success and happiness in your career, and helps create and maintain positive relationships between the shelter and the community.

▶ Youth Care Workers as professionals

Your decision to become a Youth Care Worker involves a commitment to work with troubled children. As a professional, you provide effective treatment in the context of a warm, caring environment. This means that you must exercise discretion and sound judgment as you care for children. The needs and well-being of the children always come first, so your behavior should focus on benefiting each child, the shelter, your colleagues, and Boys Town (or the organization you work for) as a whole.

Consistent use of professional skills helps you effectively work with each child and enhances your work with parents, teachers, social workers, probation officers, and others. As a result, your professionalism benefits each child and his or her successful re-entry into family, school, and community life.

In order to better understand the importance and necessity of professionalism in a shelter program, we must look at each of the nine behavior areas listed earlier.

1. Conscientious implementation of the program

"A person's conscience, like a warning line on the highway, tells them what they shouldn't do – but it does not keep them from doing it."

Frank A. Clark

Working in a shelter with many troubled children can be very stressful and hectic. However, by conscientiously implementing all components of the program, you can develop a warm, caring shelter atmosphere that is comfortable, well-organized, and pleasant. Some key concepts that are helpful in developing a positive environment include:

- Daily emphasis on program implementation and treatment goals for children.

- Efficient scheduling and time management.

Daily emphasis on program implementation and treatment goals means that each day, you are counseling, using the Motivation Systems, having Daily Meetings, and most importantly, teaching each child what he or she needs to know to grow and develop physically, intellectually, spiritually, and emotionally. (Motivation Systems and Daily Meetings will be discussed in later chapters.)

In order to help a shelter run smoothly, you need to routinely and promptly attend to daily and weekly tasks, meetings, and commitments. You will have kids to drop off and pick up, groceries to buy, and meetings to attend; efficient scheduling and time management are essential. "You've got to keep the schedule for the good of everybody," one Youth Care Worker said.

2. Appropriate modeling

"Children need models more than they need critics."
                                    Joseph Joubert

As a professional, you are a role model for your youth and colleagues. By using behaviors that are generally acceptable to society and other professionals, you show your respect for others, improve your ability to work effectively on behalf of children, and provide a good example for youth in your care. When you model appropriate behavior, it is more likely that youngsters will imitate and learn such skills as using humor appropriately, appropriately expressing anger, showing sensitivity toward others, etc. One Youth Care Worker put it this way: "I can't ask the kids to do it if I don't do it myself."

Effective professional behaviors include appropriate dress, use of correct grammar, good listening skills, and completing tasks in a timely and satisfactory manner. Youth Care Workers show professionalism by maintaining good personal hygiene and wearing clean clothing that is appropriate for the situation. Appropriate clothing in the summer may mean shorts and a loose T-shirt, while a juvenile court appearance requires more formal clothing.

By modeling these skills, you not only are more likely to receive similar courteous treatment, but also are giving your youth an example to follow.

3. Communication and general social skills

"More is to be learned from one teacher than from two books."
                                    German Proverb

Clear, frequent, pleasant communication is a hallmark of professionalism. With this kind of communication, work can be done efficiently and smoothly. Without it, confusion and misunderstandings inhibit a productive work environment. Because Boys Town Shelters are maintained by a shift staff, good communication is vital. Without good communication, one shift may not know how a youth behaved during an earlier shift or what a youth should be doing during the next shift.

Organizations, as a whole, establish a groundwork for communication through policies and procedures. Communication at Boys Town Shelters is enhanced by reading, reviewing, discussing, and following shelter policies and procedures. These policies and procedures were designed to convey accepted practices to all staff so that expectations are clear and consistent.

A number of other communication skills involve "being positive" – giving people compliments, showing appreciation, giving feedback, supporting criticism with solutions, etc. Others respect this positive "can do" attitude.

Courtesy in the work environment further strengthens communication since people can focus on what is being said rather than worrying about how it is being said. General social skills play an important role in professionalism and include such basics as pleasantly greeting others, using words such as "Please" and "Thank you," listening carefully to others without interrupting, making requests rather than demands, and following through with commitments and requests.

Written communication also is used at the shelter. When communicating in writing, it's important to be legible. If someone can't read your writing, then you haven't communicated. Time is usually a factor, so it's important to be brief and specific. This saves time for you and the reader. Using appropriate grammar and language, as always, is important. These all relate to professionalism; however, they do take time and effort. For example, when your shift is over and you want to go home, it is not easy to take the time to write legibly or use appropriate English. At times, it's good to go back and read through what you've written and see if it makes sense to you. Written communication is a basic part of your work at the shelter and one that requires professionalism.

4. Confidentiality

Confidentiality is vital to the shelter program. It builds trust with the youth, their families, and staff, and it helps to establish credibility for the shelter in the community. Youth and their families come to the shelter at a very vulnerable time in their lives. It is difficult for some to place trust in others and ask for help. It is your responsibility to show them that the shelter is a confidential facility, and that no information will be shared with anyone outside the shelter setting unless authorized by the family (i.e., school officials, therapists, etc.). If a person or organization requests information about a shelter youth, that youth's parent or guardian must sign a consent form that allows the shelter to release the information. The only exception would be when a youth alleges physical or sexual abuse; then, appropriate agencies are contact-

ed immediately. Another responsibility is to role-model confidentiality for the youth at the shelter. This means not sharing information about one youth with other youth. The youth will see that they can trust you, and will see you as being fair and concerned about them.

Confidentiality among the staff also is important. One area where confidentiality is a must is when discussing the youth and their families. Obviously, you will need to share information about the youth and their families so that all staff members can be consistent in areas such as applying treatment strategies and having phone contact with a family. However, staff members must be careful about where information is shared. The best place is a private setting away from the youth and people who have no need to know.

Confidentiality also should be exercised when sharing information about a specific staff member's job performance. It helps to establish some guidelines to enhance staff cohesiveness. Again, when sharing information with a staff member about his or her job performance, it should be done in a private setting. That way, the staff member can listen to and accept your suggestions instead of becoming defensive, which is what might happen if others are around. Also, out of courtesy, the information should stay between you and the staff member and should not be shared with others. The exception would be a situation where you have to speak with a supervisor because an issue isn't resolved. (Methods for appropriately giving and receiving feedback will be discussed later in this chapter.)

5. Contact with supervisor

The Shelter Supervisor oversees the staff's work, and during the time you are at the shelter, you will have numerous opportunities to have contact with him or her. One thing to always remember is that your supervisor is there to provide support. When you are working on a shift, you must contact your supervisor about any concerns regarding the youth, shelter procedures, or program issues. It also is important to contact the supervisor in any emergency situation, such as physical aggression, suicide ideation, self-injurious acts, medical concerns, etc. This helps develop consistency with procedures and also gives you an opportunity to share information or make suggestions on how the situation should be handled.

Another area in which you will have contact with your supervisor is consultation. Consultation involves periodic meetings between you and your supervisor to discuss concerns, share ideas, set goals, develop treatment strategies, and evaluate your progress. It is a two-way street of sharing and receiving information. This will help build a strong relationship between you and your supervisor, which helps enhance your professionalism on the job.

6. Positive consumer relationships

"I shall pass this way but once."

Unknown

First impressions are usually lasting impressions. In the shelter program, you may see a consumer only once. Positive relationships with consumers are crucial to the success of any program. At Boys Town, such relationships are necessary to carry on the shelter's mission. Consumers are individuals and agencies who work cooperatively with Boys Town, or other shelter programs, to help each child. They include parents, social service agencies, school personnel, and mental health and court-related personnel. As a Youth Care Worker, you need to create and maintain good relationships with all consumers.

To ensure better treatment and follow-through, each child at a Boys Town Shelter is assigned as the "primary responsibility" of one Youth Care Worker, who must assertively advocate for best interests of the child with teachers, administrators, police, parents, and others. This advocacy must be carried out in a way that does not alienate people or close off channels of communication. That is what professionalism is all about. Advocacy defines the content of the interactions with significant others, but professionalism defines the process and style of those interactions.

When you consistently engage in professional behaviors, you are more likely to enlist the support, cooperation, and respect of consumers and other key professionals.

7. Respecting cultural diversity

Usually, youth are in a shelter for only a short time. But during this time, it is important for Youth Care Workers to understand and be sensitive to each child's family, religious, and cultural background. This sensitivity may encompass a wide range of responsibilities, from taking a youth to church to respecting a youth's cultural differences.

Learning about these differences, and presenting them to the youth as a positive learning experience is an excellent way to teach respect for others.

8. Continued development of professional skills

As society changes, the needs of children change. In this changing environment, it is important for you to keep pace and grow professionally.

To accomplish this goal there are several things that you should focus on. One is regularly attending staff meetings. These meetings provide an opportunity to discuss a wide variety of shelter issues and situations, to learn from your co-workers and supervisors, and to develop relationships in the process. These relationships can be strengthened by asking for feedback. Some of the best advice can come from those who see what you do and how you work.

Another way to enhance your professional skills is by attending workshops and conferences and reading manuals, professional articles, and journals in order to get new ideas and learn how other people are handling child-care situations. This provides a perspective on your work, and helps you keep up on new techniques and methods.

Finally, you might think about continuing your formal education. This may help you in your current position, and help you qualify for a promotion.

9. Giving and receiving feedback

Feedback is information about how a person's behavior affects other people and the environment. Feedback can be positive or corrective in nature, and can come from anyone who sees or feels the results of another person's behavior. Feedback is essential to the day-to-day care you provide. It provides information about appropriate, productive behavior, and therefore, tells the professional which behaviors and types of interactions ought to be continued. It also provides information about behaviors or interaction styles that need to be improved or changed. Giving and receiving feedback is a foundation of learning and the cornerstone of Boys Town's programs.

In the Boys Town Emergency Shelter Services program, Youth Care Workers and youngsters must give and receive feedback every day to achieve a variety of treatment goals for each youngster. Youth Care Workers also must work cooperatively and comfortably with other professionals at the shelter and in the youth's home community. This means the skills of appropriately giving and receiving feedback must become second-nature to each Youth Care Worker.

In the short-term, high-intensity treatment atmosphere of the shelter, giving and receiving feedback appropriately is so important to the professional growth and success of a Youth Care Worker that the remainder of this chapter is devoted to reviewing the importance of these skills and how they are applied.

Giving feedback

Giving feedback is very important for building relationships, sharing information, and solving problems. Good relationships are built on open communication and the mutual respect that grows out of caring enough to share sensitive information. And, giving feedback usually is necessary to find solutions to problems; ignoring problems will not make them go away.

As a Youth Care Worker, you will have numerous opportunities each day to give feedback to youth in a shelter, to other Youth Care Workers, to administrators, and to various consumers (e.g., parents, social workers) who are involved with the youngsters. Given the importance of feedback and how frequently it is used by Youth Care Workers, it is important to learn how to give feedback in a sensitive and constructive manner.

Giving feedback involves the following steps:

1. Be attentive – face the person, smile, look at the person.

2. Request permission – ask the person if now is a good time to talk about something important.

3. Begin the interaction pleasantly – start out with praise, empathy, or pleasant comments.

4. Specifically describe the situation – give the feedback in specific terms without being judgmental, personal, or emotional.

5. Give rationales – unless the reasons are obvious, tell the person why the situation or behavior is important enough to merit your feedback.

6. Discuss the situation – be open to ideas or suggestions from the person, and offer constructive alternatives or compromises as needed.

7. Thank the person for listening – let the person know that you appreciate that he or she took the time to listen and consider the feedback.

8. Consider written feedback – if the feedback is complex or lengthy, it often helps to provide written information that the person can review in more detail after you've discussed the matter.

9. Follow-up – check back to see if the feedback had the desired effect and provide further feedback as needed.

These nine steps are very helpful when giving either positive or corrective feedback. Giving feedback in this way presents the information in a tactful, pleasant, and concerned manner that makes it easier to understand and accept, and improves the effectiveness of the feedback.

Receiving feedback

Receiving feedback also requires a special set of skills. Given the importance of feedback and the difficulties many people experience in giving it, it is important for you to encourage and solicit feedback. Youth Care Workers come to realize that the only feedback that really hurts them is feedback they do not receive.

A professional is careful not to discourage the flow of information and feedback. And knowing how to accept feedback gracefully, even though it may be difficult, is crucial to your growth as a Youth Care Worker.

The steps involved in receiving feedback:

1. Be attentive – look at the person, listen carefully, nod your head and give verbal acknowledgments, take notes.

2. Ask questions for clarification – ask a few questions if it is necessary to clarify what the feedback is about, but do not interrogate or appear to challenge the person.

3. Show concern – acknowledge the person's willingness to share information with you and show your concern if a problem exists.

4. Apologize – if appropriate, apologize for any role you may have had in a problem.

5. Avoid excuses or interruptions – don't interrupt or try to explain your side of the situation while the other person is talking. Just listen and try to reinforce the person for sharing the information.

6. Discuss the situation – if the feedback is more complex and requires some discussion about how to solve a problem, ask for suggestions and concentrate on finding a constructive solution.

7. Ask for more feedback – ask the person if there is anything else you can do.

8. Reinforce the person for feedback – throughout the discussion, and at the end, thank the person for being concerned and for sharing the information with you.

9. Request future feedback – ask the person to let you know if the situation happens again.

10. Request follow-up – ask the person if you can check back sometime later to see whether the problem has been solved.

Youth Care Workers who know how to give and receive feedback in a professional, nonpersonal manner help themselves while also contributing to the success of a shelter program.

Positive feedback helps to keep a Youth Care Worker oriented to the success of the kids and the enjoyment of progress. Corrective feedback helps you solve problems and continue to develop more sophisticated skills. Both forms of feedback must be encouraged, reinforced, and responded to appropriately if the Boys Town Emergency Shelter Services program, or other shelter programs, are to succeed with each youngster in their care.

► Summary

As a Youth Care Worker, you should take pride in your professionalism. It is a sign that you are competent, knowledgeable, and well-trained, and have the desire to improve yourself and your program. Professionalism in a shelter environment also signifies that the people charged with providing care for troubled children and their families are dedicated to the goal of making a difference in the lives of others.

CHAPTER TWO

Principles of behavior

*S*heila, *who has been at the shelter for about two weeks, notices that someone has spilled pop on the hallway floor. She gets a mop and begins cleaning up the mess. After Sheila finishes, a Youth Care Worker who was watching her comes over and says, "Sheila, that was very nice of you to clean up the floor. Thanks a lot. For doing that, you may have an extra piece of pie for dessert at dinner."*

Can you identify the pattern of behavior described above?

Youngsters come to Boys Town Shelters to get help so they can change their behavior and return home or go on to other placements. But every child is different. And even though treatment techniques are rooted in the fundamental knowledge of behavior principles, they must be adapted to meet the individual needs of each youngster.

At Boys Town, the goal of our behavior technology is to make a positive difference in the lives of the children who come to us by teaching them how to learn and live happily and successfully, despite their past problems of neglect, abandonment, and abuse.

Boys Town applies the basic principles of behavior so that our children learn to choose for themselves those courses of action that are most beneficial to them and others.

Behavioral principles are the fundamental laws or assumptions concerning the nature of behavior. They attempt to define and explain the relationships between a behavior and the specific conditions surrounding the behavior. In other words, these principles are statements of the natural causes and effects of behavior.

In order to understand the principles of behavior, it is necessary to become acquainted with certain terms and definitions. The following sections provide an overview of Boys Town's behavior technology.

▶ The ABC pattern

Behavior does not occur in a vacuum. There are events in the environment that occur before and after a behavior, and they can have a major impact on the behavior. For example, in the situation at the beginning of the chapters, the spilled pop prompted Sheila's behavior of cleaning up the mess. A reward of extra dessert will possibly cause Sheila to repeat the behavior in the future. It is important to understand what happens before and after a behavior so that the behavior itself can be fully understood.

The terms used to identify these events make up the ABC pattern:

A = **Antecedents** – The events or conditions present in the environment before a behavior occurs.

B = **Behavior** – Anything a person does or says.

C = **Consequences** – The results, outcomes, or effects of the behavior.

Antecedents

The events or conditions present before a behavior occurs can be simple or complex, recent or historical. When analyzing the antecedents of a behavior, you need to pay particular attention to the who, what, when, and where of the situation – who was present, what activities were occurring, the time of day or season of the year, and the location or physical setting. Each of these alone, or in combination with the others, can set the stage for or lead to certain behaviors.

For example, behaviors like waving a flag, yelling, cheering, carrying binoculars, doing the wave, and wearing brightly-colored clothing to reflect your loyalty are certainly appropriate for a football game (the antecedent event), but would not be considered appropriate behavior for another antecedent event like church services.

As a Youth Care Worker, you need to become familiar with a youngster's history to get an idea of what and how the youngster learned before coming to the shelter. This learning history plays a role in the antecedents of current behavior.

While the antecedents for a behavior can be complex, it often is a more simple stimulus (or set of stimuli) that immediately precedes a behavior: A telephone ring immediately precedes answering the phone, a smiling face and an extended hand invite a handshake, a red traffic light at an intersection causes a driver to step on the brake.

Behaviors

What is behavior? Behavior is anything a person does or says that can be observed directly or indirectly (i.e., seen, heard, felt, touched, smelled), and measured. At a shelter, you can observe the behavior of "sweeping the floor" directly by watching as someone does it, or indirectly by seeing that a dirty floor has been swept clean. Similarly, you may observe school behavior directly by watching a youngster in the classroom, or indirectly by asking the teacher to complete a school note each day. Since behavior is observable, it can be measured and progress can be charted over a period of time.

Consequences

The events in the environment that follow a behavior can be pleasant, unpleasant, or neutral. That is, events or consequences that follow a behavior can be classified as reinforcing, nonreinforcing, or having no effect. Reinforcing events that follow a behavior increase the chances that the same behavior will occur again in the future. Nonreinforcing events decrease the likelihood that the behavior will occur again. So, knowing what happens right after a behavior occurs not only helps you analyze the behavior, but also helps you predict what is likely to happen next.

For example, answering the telephone can result in a reinforcing event like talking to a friend, a handshake can lead to a reinforcing social interaction, and stopping at a red traffic light can lead to the reinforcing event of avoiding a traffic ticket or a wreck. In each example, the behavior results in a pleasant consequence and, in each case, the behavior is likely to occur again under the same antecedent conditions.

Consequences can be natural or applied. Natural consequences are the typical outcomes of a behavior when there is no intentional human intervention. For example, scrapes and bruises often are the natural consequences of falling down on a cement sidewalk. Losing weight is the natural consequence of going on a diet.

Applied consequences for behavior are outcomes that are deliberately arranged. In the Boys Town Emergency Shelter Services program, applied consequences take the form of points that youth earn for appropriate behavior or lose for inappropriate behavior. For example, earning 1,000 points for answering math problems correctly or learning to greet a guest is an applied consequence.

As an applied consequence, the points are effective only because they can be exchanged for privileges such as snacks, TV, free time, allowance, etc. Points become "conditioned" reinforcers because they are paired with the availability of privileges. Privileges are referred to as "back-up" reinforcers because they already have proven effective in motivating youngsters. If points could not be used to purchase privileges, they wouldn't be effective as applied consequences.

But why use applied consequences such as points? Why not use natural or "back-up" reinforcers, or privileges directly?

Using applied consequences (points) is preferable to directly using natural consequences for several reasons. First, points resist satiation. This means that youth will continue to find them reinforcing over long periods of time because points represent all privileges. Repeated, direct use of a privilege to reinforce a behavior could result in satiation – the youngster grows tired of the reinforcer and it loses its effectiveness.

Second, points are readily available, or convenient. They can be delivered at any time or any place. This is not always possible with privileges.

Third, points can be given immediately. Youth Care Workers usually have to wait for an opportunity to give a privilege, but they can respond to a behavior immediately by giving points. This strengthens the cause-and-effect relationship between the behavior and the consequence, and helps youth understand the link between what they do and what happens to them.

The immediacy of points also allows Youth Care Workers to make these applied consequences very predictable. Every time the behavior occurs, consequences follow. This consistency helps the child learn new skills and behaviors more quickly.

A final advantage of using points is that they can be used in proportion to the difficulty of the skill being learned, and be given to reinforce small improvements as well as large achievements. This sensitive application helps the child learn the new behavior and experience some immediate success for his or her efforts. Eventually, the skillful use of the new behavior will be followed by positive, natural consequences.

▶ Using the ABC pattern

Understanding the ABC pattern will help clarify why a behavior is occurring. More importantly, it helps Youth Care Workers change youth behavior; using the ABC pattern can promote change in positive, effective, and efficient ways.

How do you help youth change their behaviors? First, you change the antecedents or the consequences, or both. For example, a youth who is yelled at when given an instruction (antecedent) may respond with verbal aggression. If the adult gives an instruction in a pleasant tone of voice (changed antecedent), the child is less likely to respond aggressively. Similarly, social situations can be rehearsed, and you can point out and discuss with the youngster the events, actions, etc., that are most likely to happen prior to certain behaviors. Cues and subtle signals can be worked out to help prompt appropriate behavior in public settings. In each case, the antecedent conditions have been changed to help change behavior.

Consequences also can be changed. Points can be given for each correct answer on a worksheet; points can be taken away for disruptive outbursts; pleasant comments can follow cooperative social behavior; frowns and serious voice tones can follow a mild argument. By changing the consequences of a behavior, you can affect the behavior itself.

Many uses of the ABC pattern are built into the Boys Town Emergency Shelter Services program. The challenge that you and the administrative staff face is finding the best way to use the pattern to analyze and change difficult, recurring, or unusual problem behaviors.

▶ Some principles of behavior

As noted earlier, principles of behavior are the fundamental laws concerning the nature of behavior. They specify the relationships between behavior and the specific circumstances surrounding the behavior. Some principles of behavior are especially important as you go about the task of changing behavior.

In a shelter, Youth Care Workers use "positive reinforcement" to increase appropriate behaviors. They use a method known as "response cost" to decrease inappropriate behavior, and processes called "generalization" and "discrimination" to bring behavior under the control of appropriate antecedent events. Each of these principles of behavior is discussed on the following pages.

Positive reinforcement

Positive reinforcement means providing positive consequences immediately after a behavior in order to increase the likelihood that the behavior will occur again in the future. These consequences are intended to "reinforce" a behavior (i.e., make it stronger). Positive reinforcement, which can occur with natural or applied consequences, is used to maintain appropriate behaviors or cause them to occur more often.

The following conditions can affect how well positive reinforcement works:

1. Choose the right reinforcer. Consequences must be individualized to ensure that they actually are reinforcers for youth. Using consequences that a youth does not care about probably won't provide any incentive for him or her to change a behavior.

- Some positive consequences are social rewards like smiles, hugs, praise, and attention.

- Other possible reinforcers are "exchange rewards," like money, stars, check marks, and points that can be delivered immediately and exchanged

by the youth later for privileges or goods of some kind.

- Other positive consequences include participation in activities such as games, movies, playing outside, and watching television.

Obviously, you can determine whether a positive consequence is a reinforcer by observing the effect it has on a youngster's behavior. If the behavior occurs more often or improves, you chose the right reinforcer.

2. Deliver the reinforcer immediately. To be most effective, reinforcers need to be given immediately after the behavior you want to reinforce. The longer the time between the behavior and the delivery of the consequence, the less effective the reinforcer is in strengthening the behavior.

Points are such an effective consequence because they can be given right away when a youth displays appropriate behavior. The youth knows he or she can exchange the points later for the real or "back-up" reinforcers of privileges.

3. Choose the right amount of reinforcement. The size of the consequence should fit the behavior. Behaviors that take a long time to complete, or are difficult or new to a youth warrant a larger reward. For example, you may give a new youth a thousand points for greeting a visitor appropriately; another youth who has been at the shelter for two weeks may receive only social praise or a few hundred points for using the same skill.

You can tell whether you have chosen the right amount of reinforcement by observing the behavior of the youth. If behavior is improving or positive behavior is being maintained, then you have used the right amount.

4. Deliver reinforcers contingent on behavior. This means telling a youth, "If you do this behavior, then you will receive this consequence." This helps the youth understand that receiving a consequence depends on whether he or she behaves a certain way. You must be careful to make positive consequences contingent upon positive behavior. You also should analyze negative behaviors to determine whether any contingent rewards are reinforcing those behaviors.

5. Vary the use of reinforcers. If certain consequences are used too often, they can lose their effectiveness. One piece of candy can be a reinforcer, but a whole bag may lead to satiation and not be as effective. Watching a 30-minute show on TV may be a reinforcer, but watching TV for three hours may not be.

The possibility of satiation also means that you should use reinforcers when they are most in demand. Earning a snack an hour before dinner is much more reinforcing than earning one an hour after dinner. Watching TV when the latest rock video is on may be more reinforcing than watching TV when the news is on. You can make positive consequences most effective by using a variety of reinforcers, and by using those that are most in demand by a youngster at the moment.

6. Use schedules of reinforcement. Two basic schedules are used to deliver reinforcers to youngsters. One is a "continuous" schedule, where a reinforcer is provided every time a desired behavior occurs. A continuous schedule is very useful when teaching a new behavior. You should reinforce a youngster each and every time a new behavior is observed in order to strengthen and encourage that behavior.

After a youth has learned a behavior, an "intermittent" schedule of reinforcement can be used. On an intermittent schedule, reinforcers for a desired behavior are delivered occasionally, not every time. Reinforcers can be provided every other time or every third time the behavior occurs, or the first time the behavior occurs each hour, or on any other schedule based on frequency or time.

It seems a little illogical, but intermittent schedules of reinforcement actually are more effective than continuous schedules in strengthening behaviors. Intermittent schedules help to fade the consequences to a more reality-based schedule, where reinforcers are not provided each time a youngster does something well.

Response cost

Response cost means taking away a positive reinforcer when a certain behavior occurs in order to decrease that behavior. Losing positive reinforcers could be viewed as punishment. However, punishment usually involves the use of some aversive stimulus. (Using aversive stimuli of any kind is not allowed in any of Boys Town's programs.) Response cost is different in that it takes away something positive, rather than adding something negative.

The same conditions that affect the effectiveness of positive reinforcement also can affect response cost: immediacy, choice of the reinforcer to be taken away, amount of the reinforcer withheld, and withholding the reinforcer contingent on behavior. Many of these conditions are built into the Motivation Systems (Chapter 12) in Boys Town Shelters. Still, Youth Care Workers must consider them as they make the most effective use of consequences with each youngster.

Aversive response costs are prohibited at Boys Town. These include any type of corporal punishment, restitution, or costs that might violate a youth's rights (e.g., nourishment, communication, isolation, etc.). This not only protects you as a Youth Care Worker, but also helps the youth view the shelter as a safe place.

Generalization

Generalization means that a skill learned under one set of antecedent conditions can be used under different antecedent conditions. Basically, skills learned at a shelter can be applied in other appropriate environments outside the shelter. This means that a skill does not have to be retaught in each new environment in order for a youth to know how to use it in different environments.

Generalization can be promoted by having the youngsters thoroughly practice each skill under conditions that are as similar as possible to their environments outside the shelter (e.g., home, school, recreation area). You also can actively promote generalization by monitoring how children behave in a variety of environments. This monitoring may occur through notes from home or school,

phone calls, or information provided by other youth. This feedback allows you to reinforce youth for using appropriate behaviors in new settings.

Discrimination

Discrimination – the opposite of generalization – means that changes in the antecedent conditions produce changes in behavior. In other words, behaviors occur only under certain circumstances but not under other, different circumstances. For example, a youth who shouts in a gymnasium but who is quiet in church has learned to discriminate between these behaviors according to the antecedents. Similarly, youth must learn that aggression that is appropriate in an athletic contest is not appropriate at home, and that greeting skills used with adults are different than those used with friends.

Much of the teaching you do as a Youth Care Worker not only helps the youth learn new skills, but also teaches them where and under what conditions certain behaviors are appropriate. Teaching youth to know when certain behaviors are appropriate or inappropriate is crucial; they must learn to recognize the environmental cues that call for different behaviors.

Operant conditioning

Operant conditioning refers to the learning that occurs each day as the principles of behavior work in our environments. This learning may or may not be planned or thought out; like gravity and other natural forces, it is just there. The principles of behavior are at work every day, shaping our behavior through a never-ending stream of antecedents and consequences. Operant conditioning explains a lot of what we learn and how we behave.

On the other hand, you can utilize the principles of behavior to help the youngsters make dramatic, positive behavior changes.

Understanding the principles of behavior helps you to better understand why youth get into trouble, why they become depressed, why they have emotional outbursts, and why they are deficient in many of the skills that are necessary for normal development. This understanding can help you see how misplaced contingencies, inconsistent consequences, and unpredictable environments could shape a youngster's inappropriate behavior. Many of the youth who come to shelters are victims of an environment that reinforces many inappropriate behaviors.

Operant conditioning works both ways. Depending upon the environment, it can shape appropriate or inappropriate behavior. Many shelter youth have learned that when faced with certain antecedent conditions, they should respond with certain (often inappropriate) behaviors to get a lot of positive consequences and no negative consequences. It becomes automatic. A parent says "No" and the youth shouts "Why not?" The shouting is reinforced by attention from the parent, who tries to explain why not or gives in to the angry child. A teacher makes a request and the youth pouts and sulks. The teacher reinforces the pouting and sulking by trying to coax the youth into responding.

As important as it is to understand how kids may have learned to behave the way they do, a Youth Care Worker cannot stop there. You must intervene and try to reverse the learning that has occurred prior to their arrival at the shelter. You must interrupt the automatic behavior and get the kids to stop and think about what they are doing.

You also must harness the natural forces of operant conditioning and thoughtfully use the principles of behavior to teach the youngsters alternative, more appropriate behaviors. This gives the kids options. With options, the kids can stop and think, then choose the behavior they want. If you can teach your shelter youth to think and solve problems rationally, and teach them lots of behaviors so they have choices, then you have done your job.

Other principles of behavior also are used at the shelter. Many of these are used only under the direction and close supervision of administrators.

► Summary

Understanding the principles of behavior is the foundation of teaching new, appropriate behaviors to the youth in your care. Learning to identify and predict the antecedents that precede certain behaviors, and recognizing how powerful consequences (when used as reinforcers) can be, are integral parts of effective teaching.

While based in a behavioral technology, it is important that these principles are adapted and applied to meet the individual needs of each youth who comes to a shelter. Developing an expertise in the basic principles of behavior, their application in a shelter setting, and their integration in the teaching process is a major step toward becoming a successful Youth Care Worker.

Observing and describing behavior

Bill, a Youth Care Worker at a Boys Town Shelter, gives Bob an instruction to do his laundry. Bob looks at Bill with a sneer and says, "No way." Bill observes the behavior, then describes it back to Bob: "I know it is difficult to follow instructions, Bob, but when I gave you the instruction to do your wash, you looked at me, sneered like this, and said, 'No way.'"

A major component of effectively teaching youth is the ability to observe and describe behavior. To acquire this skill and become proficient at it, Youth Care Workers must know what behaviors to observe, how to describe them, and how being specific enhances each step of the teaching process.

This chapter explains the importance of observing and describing behavior and the role they play in the Teaching Interaction®, the nine-step process that is used to help youth correct inappropriate behaviors. (The Teaching Interaction is discussed later in this chapter and in Chapter 10.)

▶ Observing a behavior

A person who is a skillful observer has the ability to see behaviors or events in small segments – the parts that make up the whole. These "segments" include things like body movements, comments, or noises. For example, a youth might display a subtle behavior, such as rolling his eyes or sighing, or display an obvious behavior, such as yelling or cursing. A Youth Care Worker must be able to visually identify a behavior before he or she can describe it. This also means sorting through behaviors to decide which one is the most serious and should be dealt with first. Sometimes, a youth will display so many behaviors that it will be impossible to describe them all. When this happens, a Youth Care Worker must choose from those that are most obvious.

▶ Describing a behavior

When you are describing a behavior you need to be specific, objective, and behavioral. Such descriptions should be thought of as verbal instant replays of the behavior, much like what a radio announcer uses when doing the play-by-play of a sports event.

Describing behavior in a specific manner might include repeating exactly what a youth said, or explaining a behavior the youth left out, such as not saying "Okay" or not checking back with you after completing a task. If you don't remember exactly what was said, you can start your description by saying, "You said something like...." This is less likely to cause arguments. Being specific also is important because it gives the youth a clear explanation of what was inappropriate or appropriate. The youth doesn't have to wonder what behavior you're talking about, which prevents confusion and helps ensure that your teaching will be effective.

It's important to use language that the youth understand when describing a behavior. This will vary depending on their age and intellectual ability. If you observe a behavior and describe it, but they don't understand you, then you haven't accomplished your goal. They must understand.

When describing a behavior to a youth, it is important that both of you are attentive. You should be looking at the youth

and using a voice tone that fits the situation (i.e., firm, friendly, empathetic). It's also important to be at eye level with the youth (not standing above or sitting below), and to eliminate distractions. You should ask for acknowledgment from time to time to see if the youth is paying attention and understands what you are saying.

If your behavior indicates to the youth that his or her behavior is not serious, it will be hard for the youth to listen attentively. The youth should be looking at you, sitting up straight, and answering when you ask questions. This will help your teaching to be effective and also help the youth to be more successful.

▶ Demonstrating a behavior

It is sometimes easier or more effective to demonstrate a behavior rather than verbally describe it. You must be careful not to mimic the youth or exaggerate the behavior when you use this method of description. Again, be specific when describing behaviors that were used or left out, and mirror what you observed. A good example would be explaining to a youth how to do a maintenance task, like vacuuming the carpet.

▶ Being objective and behaviorally descriptive

Being objective is as important as being specific when describing a behavior. *Webster's Dictionary* defines objectiveness as "not being influenced by emotion or personal opinion." Youth sometimes will engage in behaviors to the point where you've "had enough," or they will strike a nerve by engaging in behavior that they know really bothers you. In these situations, it is extremely important to be objective and not become personally involved. Avoid using emotional terms like "bad attitude," "moody," or others that interject a personal opinion. The youth will tend to view you as being fair, and will be more likely to accept what you're saying.

Being behaviorally descriptive means describing only what you see and hear. This is important for two reasons. First, you may think you know what a youth is feeling, and sometimes you might even be right. But when you jump to conclusions based on your perceptions, rather than on what you see or hear, you run the risk of raising issues that don't need to be discussed. This can detract from the issue you should be addressing. Second, when you deal with what you see and hear, it is easier for the youth to know what your expectations are and to meet those expectations because you're describing behaviors and not feelings.

When Youth Care Workers are specific, objective, and behaviorally descriptive, the youth are more likely to know what behaviors are acceptable and what behaviors are unacceptable. Also, relationships between Youth Care Workers and youth are more apt to develop, because staff are avoiding judgmental terms and because youth view the staff as being concerned. Studies also show that youth prefer to be shown exactly what to do and how to do it.

▶ Labeling skills

The skills that are taught in Boys Town Shelters are made up of a series of components, or behaviors, that should be used in a set sequence. When teaching these skills, it is important to label the skill itself and specifically describe each of these components. Labeling the skill helps the Youth Care Worker and the youth focus on the issue at hand, provides quick information for the youth, and helps the Youth Care Worker be more consistent. It also helps the youth more easily understand what the overall skill is.

▶ Teaching Interaction

Labeling skills and describing behavior are used in all of Boys Town's teaching methods (Effective Praise®, Chapter 8; Preventive Teaching®, Chapter 9; Teaching Interaction®, Chapter 10; Intensive Teaching®, Chapter 11).

As mentioned earlier, the Teaching Interaction is a nine-step teaching tool that is used to help correct inappropriate behavior. The nine steps are listed on the next page. By labeling skills and specifically describing behavior using this interaction, Youth Care Workers can help youngsters pleasantly learn a great deal in a very short period of time.

Labeling skills and specifically describing behavior are most important in these Teaching Interaction components: Initial Praise or Empathy; Description/Demonstration of Inappropriate Behavior; and Description/Demonstration of Appropriate Behavior. Labeling and describing also are important when providing feedback after a youth practices a skill.

The Teaching Interaction includes the following components:

Teaching Interaction

1. Initial praise or empathy

2. Description/Demonstration of inappropriate behavior

3. Consequences
   - consequence
   - positive correction statement

4. Description/Demonstration of appropriate behavior

5. Rationale

6. Requests for acknowledgment

7. Practice

8. Feedback

9. Praise throughout the interaction

The next section focuses on how to apply observing and describing skills we've discussed in this chapter to the first five components of the Teaching Interaction. An example of a Teaching Interaction is used to illustrate how skill-labeling and descriptions of behavior fit into each component; the example also includes explanations of how each component is used. By learning how to specifically describe behavior and label skills during these steps, new Youth Care Workers can establish a foundation for effective teaching.

Situation: Chris, a fairly new youth in the shelter, is watching TV. A Youth Care Worker asks Chris to help set the table. Chris sighs; he doesn't look at the Youth Care Worker but gets up and walks to the kitchen. The first five components of the Teaching Interaction might sound something like this:

1. Initial praise or empathy

Youth Care Worker: "Chris, thanks for getting right up to come help set the table. I know it's hard to follow instructions sometimes, especially when you're enjoying a TV program."

Explanation: Specific, descriptive praise was given for "getting right up...." The general skill was identified in the context of the empathy statement, "I know it's hard to follow instructions...." Whenever possible, the initial praise should be related to behaviors that are part of the skill that is being taught or praised.

2. Description/Demonstration of inappropriate behavior

Youth Care Worker: "But just now when I gave you that instruction, you sighed and you didn't look at me or say anything to let me know you heard what I said, or that you would help out."

Explanation: The skill, labeled "instruction," is repeated. The description includes not only the inappropriate behavior of sighing but also a mention of the appropriate behaviors that were not displayed (e.g., "You didn't look at me or say anything...."). Also note that the Youth Care Worker avoids vague and judgmental descriptions such as, "You weren't very cooperative..." or "You didn't seem too happy when I asked you to...."

3. Consequences

Youth Care Worker: "Please take out your point card. You earned 2,000 negative points for not following instructions. You'll have a chance now to earn some of the points back by practicing how to follow instructions."

Explanation: The use of the consequence provides an opportunity to very clearly and concisely label the skill that is the focus of the interaction. It also indicates that the youth will be able to earn back some of the points by practicing the skill. Note: The Youth Care Worker should be sure to use phrases like "Give yourself" or "You've earned" when delivering consequences, rather than "I'm taking away" or "I'm going to give you...." The former phrasing helps the youth understand that he – not the Youth Care Worker – owns the behavior and is responsible for the consequences. The negative consequence helps decrease the probability that such problem behavior will occur in the future.

4. Description/Demonstration of appropriate behavior

Youth Care Worker: "Chris let's talk about following instructions. Whenever anyone gives you an instruction, whether it's a teacher, your parents, or your employer, there are several things you need to do. You need to look at the person and answer them by saying 'Okay' or 'Sure' or something to let the person know you're listening and will follow through. Be sure to ask questions if you don't understand. Do the task and then check back with the person when you're done."

Explanation: The Youth Care Worker helps the youth generalize the skill to other situations by explaining the antecedent condition, "Whenever anyone gives you an instruction...." The Youth Care Worker provides a step-by-step, behavioral description to help the youth learn the skill. Of course, during a real interaction, the Youth Care Worker would pause frequently to ask the child if he understands, has any questions, etc.

5. Rationale

Youth Care Worker: "Chris, it is important to follow instructions because when you do, you'll be able to get back to your TV program or whatever you might be doing sooner. At home, your parents will view you as being more responsible and they'll be more likely to let you do something you enjoy."

Explanation: A rationale is a statement that shows a youth the relationship between his or her behavior and the consequence or outcomes. The Youth Care Worker can generalize the rationale to other areas of the youth's life and label the skill again. An effective rationale will usually be brief, personal, believable, and describe an immediate benefit. Giving a rationale is important because it helps a child to view the Youth Care Worker as being fair and concerned. The youth will be more likely to change his or her behavior and see the relationship between behaviors and real-life consequences.

▶ Summary

You can be a more pleasant, effective teacher by following the guidelines for observing and describing behavior: Carefully observe behaviors; label skills; describe the behaviors related to them; and skillfully integrate these techniques into the components of the Teaching Interaction.

Curriculum skills

So far, this manual has laid out some basic concepts for teaching youth how to change their behaviors. Curriculum skills – the skills youngsters need to interact and function in society – are the focus of this teaching. In this chapter, we will discuss what a skill is, give some examples of specific skills, examine why it is important to teach skills, and identify when and how they should be used. (Curriculum skills also are called social skills. We will use both terms interchangeably throughout this manual.)

By definition, a skill is a set of behaviors or components that, when combined in an appropriate sequence and manner, produce positive results for an individual. A skill may have a number of behaviors or components. For example, the skill of "Following Instructions" is made up of these behaviors: 1) Look at the person; 2) Say "Okay"; 3) Do what is asked; and 4) Check back to let the person know the task is completed. Teaching these skills is an indispensable part of your job as a Youth Care Worker, and it is important that you know and are able to identify the skills and their components.

Some basic curriculum skills and their components:

Following Instructions
1. Look at the person.
2. Say "Okay."
3. Do the task immediately.
4. Check back.

Accepting "No" Answers
1. Look at the person.
2. Say "Okay."
3. Calmly ask for a reason if you really don't understand.
4. If you disagree, bring it up later.

Accepting Consequences

1. Look at the person.

2. Say "Okay."

3. Don't argue.

4. If given instructions or suggestions on how to correct the situation, follow them.

Accepting Criticism

1. Look at the person.

2. Say "Okay."

3. Don't argue.

Introducing Yourself

1. Look at the person and smile.

2. Use a pleasant tone of voice.

3. State your name.

4. Shake the person's hand.

5. When departing, say "It was nice to meet you."

A larger list of curriculum skills can be found on the Youth Teaching Target Areas form (Figure 1). For the complete Boys Town Social Skills Curriculum, refer to the Boys Town manual entitled, *Teaching Social Skills to Youth*.

▶ Why teach curriculum skills?

There are numerous benefits and advantages to teaching youth curriculum skills.

- This curriculum of skills enables Youth Care Workers to teach youth in structured and spontaneous interactions, both individually and in groups.

- Teaching skills to youth provides positive alternative behaviors to the negative behaviors they've used in the past. It shows them another way. We not only address the negative behaviors, but also offer something to take their place.

- Skill instruction teaches youth how to interact with others in ways that are more socially acceptable and valued. This assures them a better chance of being successful at home, school, work, and in other areas of life. The youth may view this in a positive light because they see that you are trying to help them become more successful.

- Teaching curriculum skills helps Youth Care Workers address treatment issues. Youth Care Workers can help youth with specific problems or inappropriate behaviors without digging up the past or getting into why they have made certain choices. Referral behaviors are addressed by teaching the youth the positive alternative: what they should have done or can do in the future.

- Curriculum skills provide Youth Care Workers with a consistent and appropriate way to deal with the youth and their behaviors. You don't have to think up ways to handle the situation; instead, you can choose the skill that best fits the issue and teach it. This helps the youth because expectations are clear, specific, and consistent. When expectations are presented this way, the youth are more likely to understand and meet them.

Figure 1

Boys Town Shelter
Youth Teaching Target Areas

Youth Name: _____ Boys Town ID#: _____

Target Areas: Date Changed _____

1. _____   2. _____   3. _____   4. _____   _____

     _____   _____   _____   _____   _____

     _____   _____   _____   _____   _____

     _____   _____   _____   _____   _____

Motivators: _____   _____

_____   _____   _____

Academics: _____

_____

Concerns: _____

_____

BSC = Basic Skill Card   PT = Planned Teaching

BSC	PT		BSC	PT	
____	___	Following Instructions	____	___	Respecting Others/Possessions/Shelter
____	___	Accepting Criticism	____	___	Apologizing
____	___	Asking Permission	____	___	Independent Living
____	___	Reporting Whereabouts	____	___	Public Behaviors
____	___	Disagreeing With Others	____	___	Appropriate Table Manners
____	___	Rational Problem-Solving	____	___	Staying Calm
____	___	Giving Compliments	____	___	Participation in Family Conference
____	___	Accepting Compliments	____	___	Getting Along with Others
____	___	Answering Telephone	____	___	School Behaviors
____	___	Introducing Yourself	____	___	Personal Hygiene
____	___	Saying Good-bye	____	___	Volunteering
____	___	Conversation Skills	____	___	Boy/Girl Relations
____	___	Asking for Help	____	___	Sportsmanship
____	___	Accepting "No" Answers	____	___	Van Behavior
____	___	Accepting Consequences	____	___	Achievement System
____	___	Showing Sensitivity	____	___	Telling the Truth
____	___	Listening to Others	____	___	Giving Instructions
____	___	Peer Reporting	____	___	Correcting Someone
____	___	Making a Phone Call	____	___	Requesting Permission/Checking In

• Youth can generalize the skills to other situations. This means that as they become more proficient and confident in their use of the skills, they learn when and how to use them in other settings and with other people.

▶ When to teach curriculum skills

Youth Care Workers should teach all of the skills listed on the Youth Teaching Target Area form (Figure 1) during a youth's stay at the shelter. Following the initial teaching of several basic skills (Following Instructions, Accepting "No" Answers, Accepting Criticism, etc.), a youth can learn three new skills each day until the list is completed. The first time a skill is introduced to a youth, it is called Planned Teaching. Other times when skills should be taught are during Teaching Interactions, role-plays, Daily Meetings, and card conferences. These are discussed in detail later in this manual. Besides these structured times, skills can and should be taught anytime a youth's behavior is addressed. Spontaneous teaching should occupy much of your time.

▶ How to teach curriculum skills

Skills are used in many settings. There also are many teaching methods for incorporating a skill into the daily routine. We will briefly discuss some of these here. These methods will be explained in more detail in later chapters.

One of these methods is Effective Praise (Chapter 8). This type of teaching is used to recognize and reward a youth's appropriate behavior. Labeling a skill and its components are a key part of this interaction.

Preventive Teaching (Chapter 9) is used to teach a youth a new skill or to remind a youth how to use a certain skill before it is used. There are three kinds of Preventive Teaching: Preteaching, Planned Teaching, and preventive prompts. The goal of each is to prevent negative behavior. Skills and their steps are labeled in varying degrees, depending on the teaching that is used.

The Teaching Interaction (Chapter 10) is used to address a youth's negative behavior; youth are taught appropriate skills so that they can replace negative behavior with positive behavior.

When a Youth Care Worker must deal with serious negative behavior, he or she will use Intensive Teaching (Chapter 11). Again, curriculum skills are taught throughout the process.

▶ Summary

Youth Care Workers at Boys Town Shelters teach a curriculum of skills that youth need in order to be successful. Consistent, frequent teaching enables youth to learn new skills, improve skills they have difficulty with, and prepare for social interactions they will have in school, at home, or in other situations outside the shelter.

CHAPTER FIVE

Rationales

Many of the youth who come to Boys Town Shelters have never learned the relationship between their behaviors and the consequences or outcomes of those behaviors. That is why rationales are such an important part of the teaching you do as a Youth Care Worker.

A rationale, by definition, is a reason. You must use rationales to explain to youth how a behavior is linked to the consequences of that behavior. For example, the rationale for practicing a sport is that a player probably will do better in a game. The rationale for getting to work on time is that being punctual increases an employee's chances of getting a raise.

In a Teaching Interaction, a rationale is a statement that describes the possible benefits or negative consequences a youth might

receive from engaging in a certain behavior. For example, you could tell a youngster that the reason she should study hard is to improve her grades. A youth who is not getting along with other children because he is calling them names might be told that no one will want to play with him if the name-calling continues. Or, the reason a youngster should follow instructions is so that he can finish his chores quickly and have more time to talk to his friends on the telephone.

It is important to point out the benefits of appropriate behavior whenever possible during a Teaching Interaction. This shows the youth there is something to be gained by learning a skill and makes it more likely that the youth will learn what is being taught. Obviously, if a youngster does something like shoplifting, it is necessary to give a rationale that points out the possible negative outcomes. However, if negative rationales are used too often, youth could perceive them as warnings or threats: for example, "John, if you don't follow instructions, you're going to get into more trouble." Positive rationales work better to encourage appropriate behavior.

▶ Importance of rationales

Rationales are important for teaching children the relationship between their behavior and what happens to them. Many children are not aware of this relationship, according to a survey conducted by D. S. Eitzen (1974). The survey, which focused on the attitudes of predelinquent and delinquent adolescents, found that these youth often see themselves as "victims of fate." For example, if a youth is arrested for stealing a car, he or she may blame the police officers for making the arrest instead of looking at the behavior (stealing) that led to the outcome. So a rationale helps children to begin to see the relationship between their behavior and consequences.

Rationales are important for other reasons. Youth like to know how they will benefit from engaging in a certain behavior, and giving a rationale lets them know. Youth also prefer disciplinary requests that are accompanied by rationales; for example, you might say, "You can't watch television because your homework isn't finished." In addition, youth are more likely to comply with a request or an instruction if a rationale is given.

Elder (1963) found that when parents provided rationales for rules and requests, their children were more likely to be confident in their own ideas and opinions. This confidence, along with the youngsters' understanding of the relationship between their behavior and the consequences, can possibly help them make better decisions.

With regard to Teaching Interactions, Willner et al. (1977), and Braukmann, Ramp, Braukmann, Willner, and Wolf (1983) found that youth prefer those in which Youth Care Workers provide explanations as they teach alternative, appropriate skills. They found that when Youth Care Workers use rationales, youth are more likely to view the Youth Care Workers as fair and like them. So, rationales seem to be important to the youth, help them understand the consequences of their behavior, and promote fairness.

A brief note of caution: Even though rationales are very important and have many uses, you should not think that good rationales, by themselves, change behavior. A combination of all the tools we present in this manual produce real changes in the behavior of children. Rationales by themselves are not enough to change behavior.

▶ Components of rationales

Effective rationales are characterized by several elements:

1. Natural consequences are identified. Rationales should point out consequences that occur naturally as a result of a behavior. Natural consequences are those that tend to occur without human intervention, or those that are not within the youth's control. For example, "If you don't take a shower or a bath regularly, you will begin to smell...."

2. Rationales are personal to the youth. Rationales need to be geared to the individual interests of each youngster. As a Youth Care Worker, you observe the youth to determine their interests, favorite activities, and likes or dislikes. Then, rationales you give during teaching can be specially tailored to each youngster. For example, if a special TV program that a youth likes is coming on soon, you might say, "If you finish your job quickly and check back, you'll have time to watch your program." This process may not be possible for a new youth until you get to know him or her better. Here, you can rely on the point system. For example, "If you learn to follow instructions, you can earn positive points." This reliance on point system rationales should be faded out to avoid emphasizing points.

3. Rationales are specific and brief. Usually, one good rationale is enough to accomplish the teaching purposes of a Teaching Interaction or praise statement. You should be brief and to the point when providing a rationale, and avoid giving the appearance you are lecturing. Long explanations may confuse a youngster, and you are more likely to keep his or her attention with a brief, specific rationale. Kids usually don't care for lectures; they prefer rationales.

4. Rationales are believable and short-term. Rationales also must be believable, which means they must be age-appropriate and personalized for each youth. For example, you might tell a nine-year-old who enjoys playing with toy cars, "If you keep your room clean, it will be easier to find your cars and it's less likely that they will get lost or broken." But a 17-year-old girl who is concerned about her appearance might be told, "If you keep your room neat, your clothes will look neater and you'll be able to find the clothes you want quickly when you're going out."

Rationales also are more effective when the immediate, rather than long-term, consequences are emphasized. For example, an effective rationale for following instructions without arguing might be, "You will have more free time if you quickly follow instructions instead of wasting time arguing." Pointing out this short-term, believable consequence is preferable to providing a remote consequence such as, "When you have a job, you will be more likely to get a promotion and a raise if you can follow instructions."

▶ When to use rationales

The appropriate use of rationales will be discussed more thoroughly in the context of various program components and procedures in other chapters. Generally, however, rationales can be used any time teaching occurs. They enhance the teaching of social skills, and make learning more relevant and meaningful to a youth by establishing a purpose or reason for the learning.

In daily shelter life, there also will be many informal occasions for you to provide rationales. Youngsters may ask for your opinion or you may offer advice or a point of view. Including rationales at every opportunity is extremely helpful!

Briefly, rationales are used in the following shelter interactions:

1. Preventive Teaching – Rationales are used in Preventive Teaching (Chapter 9), when new skills are taught to a youngster. The steps of Initial Praise or Empathy, Consequences, and Description of Appropriate Behavior precede the rationale. These rationales point out the benefits of using the new, appropriate behavior that is being taught.

2. Effective Praise – Youth Care Workers give praise, rationales, and positive consequences to reinforce appropriate behavior as it occurs in the shelter and elsewhere. Effective Praise (see Chapter 8) is an important method that can be used to encourage youngsters to make general use of the skills being taught.

3. Teaching Interactions – In a Teaching Interaction, a rationale is given after the first four steps – Initial Praise or Empathy, Description of Inappropriate Behavior, Consequences, and Description of Appropriate Behavior – are completed. Rationales in a Teaching Interaction point out the benefits of an appropriate behavior and, possibly, the harm of an inappropriate behavior.

4. Problem-Solving – Rationales are used during problem-solving as part of the **SODAS** method. **SODAS** stands for Situations, Options, Disadvantages, Advantages, and Solutions. (See Chapter 19.) Rationales are provided when listing the disadvantages and advantages of options that could be used to solve a problem.

5. Daily Meeting – Rationales are important during Daily Meeting, when shelter youth and staff gather to discuss shelter rules and make decisions. A youth uses rationales to explain why he or she is for or against a particular decision or point of view. This participation is an essential part of learning a decision-making process. Procedures for Daily Meetings are covered in Chapter 20.

▶ **Summary**

Rationales are an important part of teaching. As a Youth Care Worker, you should use rationales that are related to natural consequences, personal to the youth, specific, brief, believable, and short-term. In addition, rationales need to fit the developmental needs and maturity of the child. If you use these types of rationales, they will prove to be effective in shaping the lives of the youth in your care.

Remember, though, that rationales are most effective when used together with all the tools discussed in this manual.

Tolerances

Generally, one thinks of tolerance as a positive quality. A person who is tolerant is thought to be open to and accepting of a wide variety of beliefs, ideas, and differences among people.

When speaking of tolerance in terms of behaviors, however, the term refers to the fine line – or tolerance level – that separates those behaviors that a person will or will not accept as appropriate.

This chapter discusses the importance of setting your tolerances and expectations as you work with youth in a Boys Town Shelter or some other shelter setting.

▶ Tolerance levels

Simply put, low tolerance levels mean that very little inappropriate behavior is accepted or tolerated. High tolerance levels mean that a great deal of inappropriate behavior is accepted or tolerated.

In Boys Town Shelters, staff members are expected to have low tolerance levels for inappropriate behavior. Inappropriate behavior is a sign that a youth does not know the appropriate behavior or skill to use in a particular situation. As this manual will emphasize, alternative skills must be taught when inappropriate behavior occurs. In doing so, remember that you can set low tolerance levels and still build positive relationships. Low tolerances are important if children are to succeed and learn the skills they need to form relationships with peers and adults. High tolerance levels will not help build strong relationships and will not help the youth learn the skills they need to develop.

Whenever inappropriate behavior is allowed to occur, it tells youth that such behavior is acceptable. For example, ignoring a girl's use of sexually suggestive language and gestures tells her that these behaviors not only are socially appropriate, but also condoned by Youth Care Workers. Allowing and accepting problem behaviors inadvertently reinforces and strengthens the behavior. The least negative result is that the child is confused about what is acceptable and what is not acceptable. At worst, failure to teach more appropriate skills means that the child is "set up" for more negative or unfortunate situations, or even failure, especially when he or she leaves the shelter. In effect, the children are placed at greater risk in the community when tolerance levels are high because other adults in authority are unlikely to tolerate such problem behavior.

Low tolerances don't ensure rapid change in youth behavior. In fact, Boys Town Shelter youth usually have been reinforced for their inappropriate behavior for a long time before coming to a shelter, and it takes time to change their behavior. However, maintaining low tolerances will help you effectively and consistently convey the types of skills and behaviors youth are expected to learn.

▶ Conveying tolerance levels

From the moment a youth walks into a shelter setting, tolerance levels should be taught. The teaching procedures of the Boys Town Emergency Shelter Services program provide a specific, effective means of communicating tolerance levels by emphasizing the importance of being pleasant, positive, and specific when interacting with youth.

One way Youth Care Workers can convey tolerance levels to youngsters is through their own behavior. If Youth Care Workers model appropriate behaviors, it is more likely that the youth will engage in the expected behaviors.

Another way to convey and explain a personal tolerance level to the youth is to establish a set of shelter rules. Having clear, specific rules of behavior makes day-to-day living easier and more pleasant for Youth Care Workers and youth. Rules allow Youth Care Workers to maintain consistency as they teach youth and help them understand what is expected.

The following guidelines help determine if a behavior is inappropriate. A behavior is inappropriate if it:

- Conflicts with societal norms
- Breaks a rule in the program
- Is physically harmful to any living being
- Results in an extreme emotional outburst
- Causes discomfort or embarrassment to others (e.g., Youth Care Worker, youth, guest)
- Jeopardizes the reputation of the program
- Leads to negative consequences
- Is not appropriate for the situation

▶ Striving for consistency

Setting consistent tolerance levels reduces youth confusion, helps demonstrate expectations, and makes it easier for the youth to learn and maintain appropriate skills. Consistency also will help decrease the likelihood of tension and conflict between youth and Youth Care Workers. The youth will perceive staff members as being fair and reasonable, and positive relationships are more likely to develop and grow. Also, by frequently talking with each other about youth progress and possible inconsistencies, Youth Care Workers can work toward tolerance levels that are fairer and more consistent.

All Youth Care Workers set expectations for youth. Therefore, it is understood that patience, encouragement, and recognition should be combined with low tolerances to give youth support as they struggle to learn new ways of thinking and behaving. While it is important to have low tolerances and high expectations, recognition and praise should be given to the youth for even the smallest positive behavioral changes or efforts to master new skills.

Many of the children who come to Boys Town Shelters have been severely abused and traumatized. As a result, or as a way of coping with the abuse, they exhibit a variety of inappropriate behaviors including aggression, manipulation, withdrawal, depression, or sexual provocativeness. Youth Care Workers should not tolerate these behaviors. When they occur, alternative appropriate behaviors must be taught. It is important that tolerance levels (expectations) for abused children are the same as those for other children of the same age and development level. It is very important to be empathetic and patient and yet maintain a tolerance level that communicates compassion and concern for the child.

▶ Summary

Setting low tolerances and conveying them to the shelter youth is a key factor in successfully teaching new behaviors. Low tolerances should be consistent so that all youth understand what type of behavior is expected of them. While low tolerances and high expectations do not ensure rapid change in youth behavior, they can, when combined with praise and recognition, help youth acquire and master the new skills they need to be successful.

Reflecting on your personal tolerance levels and regularly discussing them with other Youth Care Workers or administrators are great ways to maintain appropriate, consistent tolerance levels in the shelter.

CHAPTER SEVEN

Mechanics of the point card

In Chapter 2, we talked about principles of behavior, and how we reinforce positive behavior and link a response cost to negative behavior. In this chapter, we will discuss how you, as a Youth Care Worker, keep track of these consequences and the interactions that take place.

At Boys Town Shelters, youth record the points they earn or lose each day on a point card. The card is divided into specific areas, and it is important that you understand what each area means and how it is used.

Figure 1 shows the two sides of a point card. Each area is labeled with a letter that looks like this: (A). As you read the explanation of each area, find the letter that corresponds with that area on the sample card.

Some of the terms related to the point card will be discussed in later chapters. The purpose of this chapter is to provide a general description of how point cards are used.

The front of the point card is divided into seven areas or columns. Some of these areas are duplicated on the back of the card so that more interactions can be recorded.

1. In the upper left-hand corner, there is a space for the youth's name and current Motivation System. (A)

2. The upper right-hand corner shows the codes that are used to identify Youth Care Worker numbers, target skills, the general types of behavior for which youth can earn or lose points, and whether interactions are positive, negative, or positive correction. (Positive correction is when a youth earns some points back for engaging in the appropriate alternative behavior after he or she has lost points for a negative behavior.)

YCW – This stands for "Youth Care Worker." Each Youth Care Worker is assigned a number, which is written in the column labeled "YCW" on the right side of the card. This identifies who did an interaction with the youth. **B**

SKILL – Skills are divided into three categories – social, independent living, and academic. **C**

- Social skills involve interactions with other people (e.g., following instructions, anger control, problem-solving). These behaviors are designated by a "1."

- Independent-living skills involve skills that youth must learn to be self-sufficient (e.g., cleaning, cooking, self-care, etc.). These behaviors are designated by a "2."

- Academic skills involve interactions with teachers, or school-related situations (e.g., studying, homework, class participation, etc.). These behaviors are designated by a "3."

Whenever a youth earns or loses points, the number that corresponds to the type of behavior involved is written in the column labeled "SK" on the right side of the card. **C** The goal for the distribution of points earned should be 70 percent for social skills, 20 percent for academic skills, and 10 percent for independent-living skills.

TARGET – Target skills are areas that will receive special emphasis during teaching. The target skills are recorded in the box in the upper right hand corner of the back of the card. **N** The number that corresponds with a target skill is written in the "TS" column on the right side of the card when points are earned or lost for one of those skills. **D**

+/- and PC – These symbols designate whether an interaction is positive or negative,

or a positive correction. If the interaction is positive, then the code is "1"; if a negative interaction occurs, then the code is "0." If the interaction is a positive correction (PC), the code is "2." These are written in the column marked (+/-) on the right side of the card. **E**

3. Positive Points – The number of points a youth earns is recorded in this column. Point values can vary, depending on the behavior, the youth's skill level, the frequency and intensity of a behavior, etc. **F**

4. Curriculum Skill – The name of the skill that is being taught is written in this column. The *Teaching Social Skills to Youth* manual contains an up-to-date listing of many of the skills that are part of the Boys Town curriculum (e.g., "Listening," "Following Instructions," "Disagreeing Appropriately," "Asking Permission," etc.). Chapter 4 (Curriculum Skills) also discusses these skills. **G**

5. Specific Behavior – The specific behavior or event, or the absence of a specific behavior, that earned a consequence is noted in this column. When appropriate behavior occurs, a youth earns positive points. Points are lost when an inappropriate behavior occurs or when an appropriate behavior is not used. You should use specific descriptions of behaviors to help the youth understand the appropriate and inappropriate behaviors that they engaged in. For example, the curriculum skill of "Listening" is made up of these specific behaviors: Look at the person, sit or stand quietly, think about what is being said, give an acknowledgment, and ask for clarification (if needed). Other specific behaviors such as arguing, yelling, or cursing would be inappropriate and would result in point losses. **H**

Figure 1

Name: _____ **A**

System: ❏ Daily   ❏ Achievement _____
        ❏ Assessment ❏ Other _____

	0	1	2	3	4
YCW	**B**				
SKILL	**C**	SOCIAL	INDEPDT	ACADEMIC	
TARGET	NONE	**D**			
+ / -	- **E**	+	PC		

Pos. Points	Curriculum Skill	Specific Behavior	Neg. Points	Y C W	S K	T S	+ -	YCW
F	**G**	**H**	**I**					**J**

FRONT

B **C** **D** **E**

TOTAL POSITIVES *(This Side)*   TOTAL NEGATIVES *(This Side)*

Date _____ **K** _____ **L** _____ Day _____

Name _____ **L** _____

Privileges Earned: ❏ Yes ❏ No **M**
❏ Basics ❏ Snacks ❏ TV ❏ Phone ❏ Free Time ❏ Other

TARGET SKILLS
1 _____ **N** _____ 3 _____
2 _____ 4 _____

Pos. Points	Curriculum Skill	Specific Behavior	Neg. Points	Y C W	S K	T S	+ -	YCW

BACK

TOTAL POSITIVES *(This Side)*   TOTAL NEGATIVES *(This Side)*
TOTAL POSITIVES *(Front)*   **O**   TOTAL NEGATIVES *(Front)*
TOTAL MADE   TOTAL LOST
(Minus) TOTAL LOST
POINT DIFFERENCE THIS CARD   System Standing _____ **P** _____

TARGET AREA DONE
1.
2.   **Q**
3.
4.
BSC

6. Negative Points – The number of points lost is recorded in this column. **I**

7. YCW (the column at the far right side of the card) – The Youth Care Worker puts his or her initials in this column to verify the point transaction. **J**

The back of the card contains the following:

1. Date/Day – Entering the day and date identifies the card and helps in filing and retrieving information. **K**

2. Name – The youth's name is written again to identify the card. **L**

3. Privileges Earned – Check "Yes" or "No" to indicate whether the youth earned privileges. Check the boxes next to the privileges that were earned. **M**

4. TARGET SKILLS – Curriculum skills that need special attention each day are written in these spaces. The target skills are usually identified in a youth's Treatment Plan and revised once or twice a week. You or the youngster also can use the space to note any special events or circumstances that might be in effect (e.g., "dentist appointment at 4 p.m."). **N**

5. Totals – These areas on the back of the point card help to calculate the "TOTAL MADE" (total points earned), "TOTAL LOST" (total points lost), and the "POINT DIFFERENCE THIS CARD." The Point Difference is the critical calculation that determines the number of points that are available to purchase privileges. **O**

6. System Standing – This total refers to the number of points a youngster needs to complete a particular Motivation System. **P**

7. TARGET AREA DONE – The Youth Care Worker initials this area when a youth completes a target area or a Basic Skill Card. **Q**

▶ Using a point card

Youth who are on the Assessment System or the Daily Points System use a point card. These are two of the Motivation Systems used in Boys Town Shelters. (Motivation Systems will be explained in detail in Chapters 13-16.)

Usually, each youngster carries a point card and a pen while in the shelter or with the shelter "group." This permits point transactions to occur easily and quickly. (Another option is to have Youth Care Workers carry pens.)

When a point transaction occurs, the youngster writes down the point value, the curriculum skill, and the specific behavior on the point card. The Youth Care Worker provides the information that needs to be recorded, but the youngster must write it on the card. This helps to ensure that the youth's attention is on how many points he or she has earned or lost, and the behavior that resulted in a point consequence. It also helps a youngster learn handwriting, spelling, and math skills. Younger children or youngsters who have not done well in school often need help with letters and numbers, and with spelling even simple words. For these youth, each point transition takes on extra educational dimensions.

A youngster starts a new point card during the card conference (Chapter 17) each day. After filling in his or her name, the date, day of week, and Motivation System, the youth records the privileges he or she has earned for the next day and completes the System Standing space (if needed). A Youth Care Worker reviews the card and suggests changes or approves the information before the youth leaves the card conference. During the card conference, a Youth Care Worker also should review the completed point card, praise progress toward treatment goals, discuss ways to improve on problem areas, set goals for the next day, calculate the new System Standing, and generally offer a lot of praise and encouragement to each youngster.

After the card conference, the youth can immediately begin earning or losing points. The following example provides a step-by-step description of how a youth would earn positive points from a Youth Care Worker. Figure 2 illustrates how a youth would record these points.

You are John Smith's Youth Care Worker and John is on the Daily Points System. You have just told John that he has earned 500 points for accepting a "No," answer. He writes that total in the column labeled "Positive Points." He then writes the name of the skill in the "Curriculum Skill" column, and includes a brief description in the "Specific Behavior" column.

After John records the points he earned, he asks you to sign the card. You write your assigned Youth Care Worker number in the first column marked "YCW." Next you mark the behavior as social (1), independent living (2), or academic (3) in the column labeled "SK." If John's behavior involved a target skill, you would put the appropriate number in the "TS" column. Then you would complete the (+/-) area, writing in a "1" if the

interaction was positive, a "0" if the interaction was negative, or a "2" if the interaction was a positive correction. Finally, you would write your initials in the last "YCW" column.

Figure 3 illustrates an interaction where John lost 1,500 points for not following instructions.

It is important for you to remember to keep a high positive-to-negative teaching ratio, at least eight positives or more to one negative. This helps you build relationships, and the youth tend to view you as being fair and pleasant.

At the end of each day, John "totals" the points on his card. Here is how the card in Figure 4 would be totaled up:

On the front of the card, John adds all the points in the "Positive Points" column and enters this number (10,000) at the bottom of the column in the "TOTAL POSITIVES *(This Side)*" space. He then adds all of his point losses in the "Negative Points" column and enters this number (4,500) in the "TOTAL NEGATIVES *(This Side)*" space.

John then turns the card over and totals up the "Positive Points" column on the back of the card and enters this number (7,500) in the "TOTAL POSITIVES *(This Side)*" space. Next he totals the "Negative Points" column and enters that number (0) in the "TOTAL NEGATIVES *(This Side)*" space. John then brings the "TOTAL POSITIVES" and "TOTAL NEGATIVES" figures from the front of the card, and enters these figures in the "TOTAL POSITIVES *(Front)*" space (10,000) and the "TOTAL NEGATIVES *(Front)*" space (4,500), respectively.

Figure 2

Name: _John Smith_

System: ☑ Daily ❏ Achievement _____
❏ Assessment ❏ Other _____

	0	1	2	3	4
YCW					
SKILL			SOCIAL	INDEPDT	ACADEMIC
TARGET	NONE				
+ / -	-	+	PC		

Pos. Points				Curriculum Skill	Specific Behavior	Neg. Points				Y C W	S K	T S	+ -	YCW
	5	0	0	Accepting a "No" answer	Said "Okay"					1	1	1	1	JS
				TOTAL POSITIVES *(This Side)*	TOTAL NEGATIVES *(This Side)*									

Figure 3

Name: _John Smith_

System: ☑ Daily ❏ Achievement _____
❏ Assessment ❏ Other _____

	0	1	2	3	4
YCW					
SKILL			SOCIAL	INDEPDT	ACADEMIC
TARGET	NONE				
+ / -	-	+	PC		

Pos. Points				Curriculum Skill	Specific Behavior	Neg. Points				Y C W	S K	T S	+ -	YCW
				Not Following Instructions	Didn't take shower	1	5	0	0	1	1	2	0	JS
				TOTAL POSITIVES *(This Side)*	TOTAL NEGATIVES *(This Side)*									

44

Figure 4

Name: _____John Smith_____

System: ☑ Daily ☐ Achievement _____
  ☐ Assessment ☐ Other _____

	0	1	2	3	4
YCW					
SKILL		SOCIAL	INDEPDT	ACADEMIC	
TARGET	NONE				
+ / -		-	+	PC	

Pos. Points				Curriculum Skill	Specific Behavior	Neg. Points				Y C W	S K	T S	+ -	YCW
				Not following instructions	Didn't take shower	1	5	0	0	1	1	1	0	JS
	5	0	0	Following instructions	Role-play					1	1	1	2	JS
	5	0	0	Following instructions	Took shower					1	1	1	1	JS
2	0	0	0	Accepting criticism	About muddy shoes					1	1	4	1	JS
1	0	0	0	Getting along with others	Played game with Anne					1	1	3	1	JS
				Not accepting a "No" answer	About watching a movie	1	5	0	0	1	1	2	0	JS
	5	0	0	Accepting a "No" answer	Role-play					1	1	2	2	JS
1	0	0	0	Accepting a "No" answer	About playing a game					1	1	2	1	JS
				Not getting along with others	Arguing with Jean	1	5	0	0	1	1	3	0	JS
	5	0	0	Getting along with others	Role-play					1	1	3	2	JS
2	0	0	0	Making apology	To Jean					1	1	0	1	JS
2	0	0	0	Accepting criticism	About book report					1	1	4	1	JS
1 0 0 0 0				TOTAL POSITIVES (This Side)	TOTAL NEGATIVES (This Side)	4	5	0	0					

Date _____9-18-96_____ Day _____Friday_____
Name _____John Smith_____
Privileges Earned: ☑ Yes ☐ No
☑ Basics ☑ Snacks ☑ TV ☑ Phone ☑ Free Time ☐ Other

TARGET SKILLS
1 Following instructions 3 Getting along with others
2 Accepting "No" answers 4 Accepting criticism

Pos. Points				Curriculum Skill	Specific Behavior	Neg. Points				Y C W	S K	T S	+ -	YCW
	5	0	0	Following instructions	Set the table					1	1	1	1	JS
	5	0	0	Following instructions	Cooked dinner					1	1	1	1	JS
2	0	0	0	Accepting criticism	About playing loud music					1	1	4	1	JS
1	0	0	0	Getting along with others	Played game with Anne					1	1	3	1	JS
	5	0	0	Problem-solving	Role-play					1	1	0	1	JS
	5	0	0	Accepting a "No" answer	About playing a game					1	1	2	1	JS
1	0	0	0	Getting along with others	Role-play					1	1	3	1	JS
	5	0	0	Following instructions	Role-play					1	1	1	1	JS
	5	0	0	Following instructions	Took shower					2	1	1	1	FW
	5	0	0	Conversation skills	Talked with visitor					2	1	0	1	FW

											TARGET AREA DONE
7 5 0 0	TOTAL POSITIVES (This Side)	TOTAL NEGATIVES (This Side)	0								
1 0 0 0 0	TOTAL POSITIVES (Front)	TOTAL NEGATIVES (Front)	4 5 0 0								1.
1 7 5 0 0	TOTAL MADE	TOTAL LOST	4 5 0 0								2.
4 5 0 0	(Minus) TOTAL LOST										3.
1 3 0 0 0	POINT DIFFERENCE THIS CARD	System Standing 60,000									4. BSC

After adding the positive points, he writes the total (17,500) in the "TOTAL MADE" space. John then adds the "TOTAL NEGATIVES *(This Side)*" figure to the "TOTAL NEGATIVES *(Front)*" figure and enters that number (4,500) in the space labeled "TOTAL LOST." This number is then brought over and entered in the "*(Minus)* TOTAL LOST" space directly below the "TOTAL MADE" area. The "*(Minus)* TOTAL LOST" point figure is then subtracted from the "TOTAL MADE" figure and the difference (13,000) is written in the space labeled "POINT DIFFERENCE THIS CARD."

This total is the number of points John can use to buy privileges for the next day (24 hours). Since John is on the Daily Points System and the daily difference is 10,000 positive points, he would be able to purchase the privileges for that system.

In addition to buying privileges, the positive points John earned that day also are subtracted from the System Standing total (60,000). John now starts a new point card and the new System Standing total is written on the new card.

Completed point cards are kept in the youth's file for future reference.

▶ Other cards and charts

It is important that the youth learn to use correct spelling when they are asked to write something on their point cards. It would be time-consuming for the youth to go to the dictionary every time they didn't know how to spell a word, so youth who have difficulty in this area can carry a Spelling Card that lists frequently used words.

Usually, the card contains curriculum skills like "Following Instructions," "Asking Permission," or "Accepting 'No' Answers."

Visual charts are used for youth who have difficulty understanding the point card. These charts, which can be kept on a bulletin board, are sometimes more motivating to a youth because they can include a particular area of interest like basketball or video games. Only shelter administrators can authorize use of these charts for the youth.

From time to time, youth who are on the Achievement System may have to go back on a point card for displaying serious negative behavior. The card works the same as with youth on Daily Points.

▶ Point card responsibilities

The child's role

The point card is a very important tool because it contains the day's "story" for each youth. Youth need to fill out their own cards in order to practice handwriting, spelling, and math skills. They also need to keep their cards with them at all times. This accomplishes two things. First, it is a simple instruction and it allows you to test their ability to follow instructions. Second, it makes it easier to teach any time because the card is always available. In addition, the youth should use an ink pen so interactions can't be easily erased or modified. When totaling up, it is important for a youth to do his or her own addition and subtraction. A youth who is on a point card is working on tomorrow's privileges.

The Youth Care Worker's role

Youth Care Workers need to monitor point cards for correct spelling, possible, manipulation, or honest mistakes. This is a great way to review a youth's day, praise positive behaviors or accomplishments, and identify negative behaviors that need attention. Youth Care Workers also can challenge the youth to set goals, particularly in areas of difficulty. When reviewing the day, it also is important to pay close attention to the youth's target areas to see if they are making progress.

Administration's role

Administrators are responsible for doing point card reviews. Information that is gathered allows administrators to give Youth Care Workers feedback on their teaching – the percentage of social, independent-living, and academic teaching; ratios of positive-to-negative interactions; and frequency. This review also can help administrators identify treatment concerns that need to be addressed with youth.

▶ Importance of the point card

The point card is a very important tool because it provides a record of the day. This is helpful in identifying the youth's needs and how Youth Care Workers are meeting those needs. It also provides structure to a shelter, giving youth and staff a reason to interact. The card allows Youth Care Workers to maintain consistency by setting specific point amounts for behaviors, while providing enough flexibility to modify point amounts to fit different situations.

▶ Summary

The point card is a key part of the Motivation Systems used at Boys Town Shelters. Learning how to use it so that it becomes a natural part of your teaching will help you be more effective in your interactions with youth. Your complete knowledge of the point card and the Motivation Systems also will enable you to explain to youth how to fill out cards themselves, another step toward helping them learn responsibility and independence.

Relationship-building/Effective praise

*T*ina walked into the kitchen where Chris, a Youth Care Worker, was preparing dinner.

"Look who's here!" said Chris. "The best spaghetti cook in town!"

"Thanks," Tina replied, looking a little flustered. "And thanks for helping me."

"You're welcome," Chris said with a smile. "Let's talk about how well you just accepted that compliment."

Chris is building relationships with Effective Praise.

Building strong relationships between Youth Care Workers and the children they care for is one of the keys to a successful program. Most of the children who come to Boys Town Shelters, however, have not learned how to develop positive relationships. It has not been easy for them to make and keep friends. They also have had problems getting along with adults in authority – their parents, teachers, and employers, to name a few.

Developing and nurturing relationships is a key to living a rewarding and happy life. Youngsters who have not learned this skill are missing the friendship and love they need from other people as they grow. That is why building positive relationships with the youth in your care is so critical. Not only are you teaching the youth how to develop healthy relationships with others, but you also are creating an atmosphere of trust and security between yourself and the youth. This will help you in your teaching and make it more likely that the youngsters will benefit from their experiences at the shelter.

This chapter reviews the benefits of building strong relationships, how youth can develop those kinds of relationships, and the activities, attitudes, and behaviors you can use to enhance relationship development.

▶ Building strong relationships

Many components work together when people are building strong relationships. In shelters, two key components are discipline and interpersonal skills. We will briefly discuss these components in this section.

Webster's Dictionary defines discipline as "training intended to elicit a specified pattern of behavior or character." In shelter care, this training takes the specific forms of teaching, which will be discussed in this chapter and in Chapters 9, 10, and 11.

Teaching in the shelter means reinforcing positive behavior and giving consequences for negative behavior. Even though you will work with youth for only a limited time in the shelter, your teaching can help them "shape" appropriate behaviors and develop the skills they need in order to build strong relationships.

The first step to teaching is being able to identify teaching opportunities. Youth Care Workers must be able to recognize the types of behaviors they should respond to, and then respond appropriately. For example, if you ask a youth to take out the garbage, and he completes the task right away, you should reinforce that positive behavior with some type of positive consequence. Second, it is important to not avoid addressing negative behavior. Sometimes, it might be easier for you to look the other way. Or you may want to excuse misbehavior as a way of showing that you are sympathetic and understand the problems a child has faced. You also may feel like ignoring misbehavior because you don't want to deal with the youth's negative response to your teaching. When this happens, the youth has taught you not to respond by making the cost of teaching too high. In these situations, you need to remember that you are a teacher, not a punisher, and that to ignore a behavior is to pass up an opportunity to teach. This isn't fair to you or the youth.

Also, in learning how to build relationships, youngsters must understand that there are certain behaviors that you, and others, find acceptable or unacceptable. We defined this earlier as a tolerance level (Chapter 6).

A second component of building strong relationships is interpersonal skills. These include qualities that both you and the youth enjoy, like a good sense of humor, openness, listening attentively, communicating clearly, being trustworthy, and showing sensitivity. The youth you work with usually will not have many of these qualities when they first come to the shelter. It is your responsibility as a Youth Care Worker to teach these qualities and help the youth develop them. Remember that relationships are based on the way people interact with each other.

Research has identified the following Youth Care Worker behaviors as those that are liked and disliked by youngsters in group homes (Willner et al., 1977).

Liked behaviors

1. Calm, pleasant voice tone
2. Offering or providing help
3. Joking
4. Positive feedback
5. Fairness
6. Giving points
7. Explanation of how or what to do
8. Explanation of why (giving rationales)
9. Concern
10. Enthusiasm
11. Politeness
12. Getting right to the point
13. Smiling

Disliked behaviors

1. Describing only what youth did wrong or not offering initial praise for what was done correctly
2. Anger
3. Negative feedback
4. Profanity
5. Lack of understanding
6. Unfriendly
7. Unpleasant
8. Bossy or demanding
9. Unfair point exchange
10. Bad attitude
11. Unpleasant physical contact
12. Mean, insulting remarks
13. No opportunity to speak
14. Shouting
15. Accusing, blaming statements
16. Throwing objects

"Liked" behaviors let the child know that you are sincere and are truly concerned about the youth. Quality components contribute significantly to the quality of the interaction.

►Benefits of building strong relationships

There are numerous benefits for developing and maintaining strong, personal relationships with each youth in a Boys Town Shelter. In general, strong relationships between you and the youth enhance your ability to help bring about changes in each child's life, create a more pleasant shelter environment, and improve the effectiveness of the overall program and the benefits for each child. Strong relationships contribute substantially to your ability to help each child learn and grow. When relationships are healthy and strong, the youth are more likely to spend time with you. When youth seek you out and want to be with you, the entire teaching and learning process is greatly enhanced. That means you will have many more opportunities to teach by example as children spend more time in the presence of positive, adult role models.

Furthermore, as relationships develop, youth are more likely to identify with and accept your values, rationales, and opinions. In this way, youth can receive the biggest benefit from you as a positive role model.

In addition to making your role-modeling more effective, good relationships can improve the youngsters' receptivity to more direct teaching. That is, youth are more likely to accept your feedback, whether it takes the form of a compliment or a complete Teaching Interaction, to correct an inappropriate behavior.

The youth who come to Boys Town Shelters need the benefit of positive role models and active help through teaching, as well as being able to talk with you about how they are feeling and what they are thinking. With a sensitive relationship to rely on, a youth is much more likely to communicate frequently and honestly with you. With frequent, open communication, it is easier for you to be sensitive to the needs of each child and to individualize the program so that it can accomplish what is best for each child.

As youth develop close ties with you, they begin to care about your opinions of them. In essence, your approval and view of the youth become reinforcers for them. It is hoped that, over time, youth will come to care about these opinions and want the approval of other important role models and significant others such as clergy, teachers, parents, etc.

►Effective Praise

Effective Praise is crucial to developing relationships and strengthening appropriate behavior. Effective Praise Interactions enable you to sincerely and enthusiastically recognize the progress each child is making. How the praise is given makes it effective in developing relationships and in reinforcing behavior. Effective Praise includes the following components:

Effective Praise

1. Praise
2. Description of appropriate behavior
3. Rationale
4. Request for acknowledgment
5. Positive consequence

The following is an example of an Effective Praise Interaction:

Situation: You and Joe have just reviewed Joe's point card. It was not the best day Joe ever had, and while there were several positives to review, there also were a number of problems to discuss. Joe has accepted the criticism very well.

1. Praise

Example: "Joe, that was great and so impressive. You have really come a long way in learning to accept criticism."

2. Description of appropriate behavior

Example: "When we reviewed the problem behaviors that were listed on your point card, you really handled it well. You looked at me as we talked, you calmly said 'Okay' to let me know you understood, and you didn't argue, raise your voice, or make excuses. Great job!"

3. Rationale

Example: "When you accept criticism from people, you can learn a lot and avoid creating more problems. I know you're really looking forward to playing basketball, but the coach needs to criticize your playing to help you improve. If you can handle his feedback as well as you've handled this criticism, you'll probably spend more time playing and less time on the bench."

4. Request for acknowledgment

Example: "Does that make sense?" or "Do you understand what I mean?"

5. Positive consequence

Example: "You've earned 2,000 points for accepting criticism while reviewing your point card."

In summary, the use of Effective Praise not only builds relationships but also increases the probability that the appropriate behavior will occur again in the future.

▶ Teaching Interaction

It may seem like a difficult and contradictory task to be frequently teaching and correcting children and still be developing strong relationships with them. However, because relationships are based on how people interact with one another, you can develop positive relationships and teach. First, though, you have to know how to teach. Relationship development does not depend on whether or not you teach and correct problem behaviors, but how the teaching is accomplished.

If you correct problem behaviors by using the Teaching Interaction, you are engaging in a number of behaviors that help build relationships. In fact, five of the nine Teaching Interaction components are relationship-building components. The following is a list of the Teaching Interaction components. The asterisks indicate the components that enhance relationships between you and the youth, even when you are correcting problem behaviors.

1. Initial praise or empathy *

2. Description/Demonstration of inappropriate behavior

3. Consequences
    – consequence
    – positive correction statement *

4. Description/Demonstration of appropriate behavior

5. Rationale *

6. Requests for acknowledgment

7. Practice

8. Feedback *

9. Praise throughout the interaction *

Praise or empathy, positive feedback after the practice session, and praise throughout the interaction all contribute significantly to developing a positive relationship. By recognizing a youth's progress (even the smallest bit of progress) and using genuine words and gestures of encouragement, you show that you care about the youngster and that you are aware of his or her efforts. Praise builds relationships.

A situation in which a youth earns a negative consequence might be perceived as one that can damage a relationship. But, by offering a positive correction statement with the consequence, you let the youth know that he or she will have an opportunity to earn back up to half of the points that were lost. This helps build relationships because it shows the youth that you are fair and concerned about his or her success.

Rationales also are a key relationship builder. Children appreciate being told why a behavior is appropriate. It shows them that you are not arbitrary or capricious, and that you have their best interest at heart.

▶ Other elements of a positive relationship

Of course, there are a number of other activities and behaviors that Youth Care Workers can engage in to build relationships with their youth. You can create the opportunity to build relationships simply by spending time with your youth. Time spent in recreational activities, talking together, or working alongside the youth is a great way for you to get to know them.

Because shared experiences and "remember when" times are important for relationship development, Youth Care Workers and the youth in Boys Town Shelters regularly plan and attend a variety of activities. Such activities can range from an evening of bowling to an in-house contest (e.g., dancing, board games, bake-off, etc.). Of course, holidays, birthdays, and outings provide special opportunities to develop closer relationships as events are planned and enjoyed.

You also develop close relationships by displaying concern for the happiness and well-being of each child. That means doing Preventive Teaching with each child to ensure that he or she has the necessary skills to get his or her needs met. (See Chapter 9.) You are there to listen when a youth needs to talk and to be sensitive to the child's feelings and background.

In the midst of the structure provided by the program, there is room for and a need for flexibility, as well. You need to ask youngsters for input, allow them to help plan activities, be open to their concerns and criticism, and in general, reinforce the notion that the shelter truly is a "home."

Finally, relationship development is an important part of dealing with problem behavior. As noted earlier in this chapter, several components of the Teaching Interaction deal with serious misbehavior. Youth Care Workers should use large amounts of empathy and praise to maintain and continue to develop positive relationships even during those difficult times.

▶ Summary

Building strong relationships with the youngsters in your care may be the most important aspect of the Boys Town Emergency Shelter Services program. That's because good relationships allow you to accomplish so many other goals. Relationships make your teaching effective and help create a pleasant atmosphere for youth and Youth Care Workers alike. Above all, building positive relationships shows youngsters that you care about them and what happens to them.

CHAPTER NINE

Preventive teaching

Developing relationships with youth through teaching is always a priority in a Boys Town Shelter. Among the variety of teaching methods Youth Care Workers can use is one called Preventive Teaching. As part of a proactive approach to providing treatment, Preventive Teaching occurs frequently to promote the development of new skills, to prevent problems from occurring, and to increase each youth's opportunities for success. This teaching technique involves identifying skills a youth needs to learn, planning an instructional session to teach the skills, and conducting the teaching session.

The notion of "prevention" is not unique to the Boys Town Emergency Shelter Services program; it is a concept that is important in society in general. One example of preventive teaching is a fire drill. Fire drills involve having the occupants of a building practice locating alarms and extinguishers, and using exit routes. Such preventive teaching reduces the chances of serious injury or death that might result from a real fire. Another example of preventive teaching is taking a young child on a "safe walk" to and from school at the beginning of the school year. During this walk, the parent can teach the child the route and how to cross streets safely, and can point out "block homes" along the route where children can go for assistance. Such preventive teaching improves the child's safety and reduces anxiety for both the child and the parent. By taking the opportunity to review and teach to situations that will occur in the future, problems can be prevented when these situations arise.

Preventive Teaching in Boys Town Shelters provides similar benefits to youth and Youth Care Workers. Many of the boys and girls who come to Boys Town Shelters have experienced a great deal of criticism and very little success. Preventive Teaching provides an excellent opportunity for Youth Care Workers to reverse that process. It not only improves the child's chances of succeeding, but also provides Youth Care Workers with more opportunities to teach. Those preventive opportunities are likely to be successful and beneficial because they are occurring when a youth is not displaying problem behaviors. Anxiety levels and emotions are under control, and the learning process is made easier because of the comfortable, supportive, relaxed environment.

Preventive Teaching is a great relationship builder. Youth appreciate the inherent fairness, concern, and support involved in learning something new that will benefit them in the future. They also appreciate the opportunity to learn how to avoid using inappropriate behaviors that will result in more difficulties for them. Their anxiety will be reduced when they need to use a particular skill or behavior, and they can more confidently approach new situations, as well as recognize and correct previous problems. In effect, they have the opportunity to experience success without ever having experienced failure!

It is essential that Youth Care Workers set youth up for success and show staff tolerances through Preventive Teaching. This is especially important in a short-term setting like a shelter. In order to quickly orient youth to their new surroundings, Youth Care Workers should use Preventive Teaching frequently with new youth.

▶ Why teach preventively?

A preventive approach gives youth the opportunity to comfortably succeed, and enhances the success of the Youth Care Workers. Indeed, your job satisfaction and personal satisfaction is improved as a result of effective Preventive Teaching. Preventive Teaching also helps Youth Care Workers avoid confrontations by positively and preventively establishing expectations and developing the youth's skills. And although you are always monitoring behavior, you can be more relaxed and comfortable with your youth in a wide variety of situations.

The practical application of Preventive Teaching techniques involves knowing what to teach, when to teach, where to teach, and how to teach. In terms of content, sessions can focus on basic curriculum skills, advanced curriculum skills, or preparation for a specific set of circumstances (i.e., a child going home after his or her stay in the shelter). When youth enter the program, they must learn about Boys Town Shelters. The teaching agenda involves basic curriculum skills the youth need as they live in the shelter and information about Boys Town Shelters as a spiritual, social, and educational community: What are the program expectations? How do people in the shelter live together? What's going to happen when they leave the shelter?

The use of Preventive Teaching continues as the youth advance through the program. The focus may shift from teaching basic skills to teaching more advanced skills and preparing youth for their future.

The basic curriculum skills taught to youth during their first few days at a Boys Town Shelter include "Following Instructions," "Accepting Criticism," "Accepting 'No' Answers," "Asking Permission," "Accepting Consequences," and rational problem-solving. Preventively teaching these skills helps the youth become open to and comfortable with the process of learning new skills.

Learning new skills is frequently reinforcing in and of itself, so the teaching process itself becomes reinforcing. In effect, having the youth learn and master these basic skills makes it easier to teach. Having children learn these basic skills sets the stage for teaching more advanced skills, such as being honest, helping others, being sensitive to others, finding a job, etc.

These basic and advanced skills help the youth develop a wide variety of family and community-living skills. Most children receive a gradual "education" in these skills from their parents and other adults through modeling, discussions, praise, and discipline. The children at Boys Town Shelters (by and large) have not been a part of such a natural, prosocial education process. In fact, most youth have received an inconsistent and often dysfunctional education that has left them confused and socially inept. Frequent, specific Preventive Teaching is critical if these youngsters are to make up for lost time and lost opportunities.

In addition to teaching frequently used basic and advanced curriculum skills, you also will preventively teach the youth how to behave under specific or special circumstances. Usually, Youth Care Workers are able to identify such circumstances because they know each child's strengths and weaknesses, and anticipate situations that call for Preventive Teaching. For example, if a youth's parent will be visiting him or her at a Boys Town Shelter, you would preventively teach a number of social skills. Such skills might include getting along with adults, greeting someone, and how to engage in a conversation. Or, a youth who has always had difficulty asking permission and accepting "No" answers from his parents may be going home for the evening. In that case, you would focus on those skills in order to prepare the youth for a more successful home visit. In both cases, Preventive Teaching improves the youth's opportunity to succeed.

Preventive Teaching also is helpful in avoiding confrontations or situations that result in an out-of-control emotional response by the youth. For example, if a youth becomes verbally or physically aggressive, or loses self-control when told "No," you should focus a great deal of Preventive Teaching on that skill. This type of teaching should occur before a youth encounters the antecedent conditions that spark such behavior, and in the absence of such conditions. Preventive Teaching can be used to teach any skill and to prepare for potentially difficult situations.

Another advantage of Preventive Teaching is that it can occur privately with individual youth, in small groups, or with the group as a whole.

When working privately with one youth, concentrate on specific treatment goals or special situations the youth must face. Small or whole group sessions typically focus on skill areas that are common to all youth.

For example, if the group will be attending a particular social event, the Youth Care Workers may choose to review manners, conversation skills, and expectations for the youth during the outing. Such group teaching allows the Youth Care Workers to efficiently teach necessary skills.

▶ Types of Preventive Teaching

There are three types of Preventive Teaching. They can be used at various times and in different settings.

One type of Preventive Teaching is Planned Teaching. Planned Teaching is used when a youth is learning a new curriculum skill. This method is used to teach basic skills at first, but may be used with more advanced skills as the youth makes progress. Planned Teaching should be done in a neutral setting and practice scenarios should be realistic and apply to situations the youth will encounter.

Planned Teaching involves the following steps:

Planned Teaching

1. Introduce the skill
2. Describe appropriate behavior
3. Give rationale
4. Request acknowledgment
5. Practice
6. Provide practice feedback
7. Positive consequence
8. Follow-up sessions

As you begin the sequence, clearly label and explain the skill that will be taught. You can then review a number of specific examples of how the skill is used, and give the youth opportunities to ask clarifying questions.

Next, specifically describe the appropriate behaviors that make up the skill. Demonstrating the skill is a good way to describe it.

The third step is giving a rationale that explains to the youth why it is important to use the skill. After the rationale, you should ask the youth if he or she understands and ask for acknowledgment. (A Youth Care Worker can ask for acknowledgment and answer questions anytime during the interaction.)

After you describe the appropriate behavior, provide the rationale, and request acknowledgment, the youth should practice the skill. This helps the youth become comfortable with it and enables you to determine how well you are teaching. It is important that the youth practices the skill correctly. If a step is missed or you don't like the practice for some other reason, have the youth practice again. Remember that when a youth practices a skill incorrectly, he is learning inappropriate behavior.

When the practice is completed, provide feedback to the youth using sincere, descriptive praise for all appropriate behaviors, and deliver positive points for the practice session.

The new skill can be further reinforced through a series of follow-up practice sessions. You should tell the youth about these practice sessions, and have the first one soon after the Planned Teaching Interaction. After each practice, you can continue to provide descriptive praise, descriptions of appropriate behavior, and positive points.

The second type of Preventive Teaching is called Preteaching. Preteaching is used to review how to use a skill just before a situation in which a youth will actually need to use it. For example, a youth who already has been taught the skill of "Accepting 'No' Answers" comes up to a Youth Care Worker and asks to play pool. Before saying "No," the Youth Care Worker would preteach the skill.

The steps, which are similar to those of Planned Teaching, include:

Preteaching

1. Re-introduce the skill

2. Describe appropriate behavior

3. Give rationale

4. Request acknowledgment

5. Practice (Youth Care Worker discretion)

6. Practice feedback (only if the youth practices the skill)

7. Positive consequence (only if the youth practices the skill)

8. Inform youth of the situation

The last type of Preventive Teaching is a preventive prompt. A preventive prompt is a brief reminder of a skill that should be used in a situation; it is given to a youth just before the situation occurs. For example, a youth displays poor sportsmanship by cheating during a game. The Youth Care Worker is about to have the youth earn a negative consequence for cheating. But before doing so, the Youth Care Worker gives this preventive prompt: "Do you remember the steps to accepting a consequence? What are they?" After the youth gives the steps to the skill, the Youth Care Worker delivers the consequence. Having the youth go through the skill's steps makes it less likely that he will respond to the Youth Care Worker in a negative manner because the youth has been reminded of how he is expected to behave. (You also may choose to give the skill's steps yourself.)

One other way to use a preventive prompt is to label the skill: "Sarah, do you remember how to accept 'No?'" Without naming the steps, you have reminded the youth about the skill that she should use.

Preventive prompt

1. Remind the youth of the skill

2. Describe appropriate behavior (Youth Care Worker discretion)

▶ Summary

Preventive Teaching builds relationships and fosters skill development. It is probably the most important tool a Youth Care Worker has for controlling youth behavior. It can be used to teach youth curriculum skills, as well as to prepare them for specific situations or circumstances. It can be used on an individual basis or with a group of youth, depending upon the circumstances. The three types of Preventive Teaching used at Boys Town Shelters are Planned Teaching, Preteaching, and preventive prompt.

CHAPTER TEN

Teaching interaction

The youngsters who come to emergency shelters have had a difficult time being successful at home, in schools, and in their communities. Many of them have been physically and psychologically abused. They have lived in dysfunctional and often chaotic environments. As a result, they have exhibited problem behaviors that have led them to be labeled as "delinquent," "emotionally disturbed," or "ungovernable."

But along with their problems, each child brings to a shelter his or her special strengths and qualities. The goal of the Boys Town Emergency Shelter Services program is to build on these strengths and remediate problems. Rather than viewing a child as "delinquent" or "disturbed," Youth Care Workers take the approach that youth need to learn a wide variety of skills in order to be successful.

Most children learn appropriate behaviors and skills by observing and emulating the many positive role models in their lives. Most of the youngsters who come to Boys Town Shelters have not had positive, consistent role models, or such modeling has not helped them learn appropriate behaviors and skills. Often, their "reinforcement histories" have led to behaviors that provide immediate gratification, but turn out to be very destructive in the long run.

Because these youth have so much to learn and "unlearn" in a relatively short time, the key to success is frequent, direct, skillful teaching. Teaching is the critical difference between real treatment and "warehousing." As a Youth Care Worker, you will help each child learn new skills that can replace past problem behaviors. These new skills also will help youth in their normal development as they grow through adolescence. Because children who come to a shelter are directly taught new ways of behaving, each youngster can more successfully and comfortably adapt to societal norms and get his or her needs met in socially acceptable ways.

Direct, frequent, concerned teaching also helps Youth Care Workers. Such a teaching approach provides a specific, effective, positive way to deal with problem behaviors. Because teaching is a positive approach that works well and is liked by children, you can avoid punitive approaches that would damage relationships.

For example, Martha Bedlington and her colleagues studied several group homes and found that the level of teaching in a home positively correlated with youth satisfaction and negatively correlated with self-reported delinquency (Bedlington, Braukmann, Ramp, & Wolf, 1988). That is, the more teaching the Youth Care Workers did, the better the youth liked the program and the less delinquency they reported. Youth Care Workers also benefit from teaching because as they see the progress each child is making, their commitment and sense of accomplishment grows.

In Boys Town Shelters, the nine-step Teaching Interaction is used to correct inappropriate behavior and effectively meet the individual needs of each child. By mastering this process and its components, Youth Care Workers can deal with problem behaviors and teach more appropriate alternatives. By thoughtfully and consistently using the Teaching Interaction, you can help each child recover from the past and grow into the future.

The remainder of this chapter reviews in more detail each of the nine components of a Teaching Interaction. In addition, some special techniques and applications are explained to help you successfully apply your teaching skills.

▶ Teaching Interaction components

The following nine components and the various subcomponents are used to correct problem behaviors and teach new alternative skills and behaviors.

Teaching Interaction

1. Initial praise or empathy
2. Description/Demonstration of inappropriate behavior
3. Consequences
   - Point loss
   - Positive correction statement
4. Description/Demonstration of appropriate behavior
5. Rationale
6. Requests for acknowledgment
7. Practice
8. Feedback
   - Praise
   - Specific description or demonstration
   - Positive consequences
9. Praise throughout the interaction

The following section defines and explains each Teaching Interaction component.

1. Initial praise or empathy

The best way to start an interaction on a positive note is to specifically and sincerely praise any aspect of a child's behavior that is appropriate. To ensure that the praise is effective, it should be behaviorally specific and descriptive (see Chapter 3, "Observing and Describing Behavior"), and related to the skill that will be taught. Using this type of praise makes it more likely that those particular appropriate behaviors will occur again in the future. Praising behaviors that are related to the skill or close to the interaction has two functions. First, it increases the sincerity of the interaction and makes it seem more genuine and natural. Second, it reinforces approximations to the desired behavior and helps the youth recognize progress. (See Chapter 2, "Principles of Behavior.")

If a child's behavior does not warrant praise or is not related to the skill being taught, you still can begin the interaction on a positive note by providing an empathy statement. An empathy statement lets the child know that you understand how she or he may be feeling. Examples of empathy statements might be, "Mark, I know how much you were counting on playing basketball and I'm sure you're really disappointed that you can't play," or "Boy, it can be really irritating when somebody uses your book and doesn't tell you about it." Such empathy statements can help build relationships, calm a youth who is upset, and help you approach the situation in a positive, calm manner.

When you do not consistently use this component, youth may come to view you as a punishing stimulus – someone who is quick to criticize and slow to recognize accomplishments. When the youth begin to feel this way, they may begin to actively avoid you.

By using initial praise and empathy consistently, you strengthen and reinforce appropriate behavior. You also can build relationships by recognizing accomplishments and acknowledging feelings, which helps the child become more receptive and open to the entire teaching process.

2. Description/Demonstration of inappropriate behavior

This component involves labeling the skill that is being taught and specifically describing the youth's inappropriate verbal and nonverbal behavior. Labeling the skill often is accomplished by describing the antecedent conditions (e.g., "When you greeted your caseworker Mrs. Smith..." or "When I gave you the instruction to..."). When behaviors are difficult to describe, such as voice tone, gestures, or facial expressions, you can demonstrate the behavior. However, be careful not to be sarcastic or rude.

During this step, it is important to use the skills and their components that were presented in Chapter 3, "Observing and Describing Behavior." This helps you provide clear skill labels and nonjudgmental, specific behavioral descriptions. Clear descriptions of inappropriate behaviors help the youngster understand exactly what behaviors need to be changed. The youth doesn't have to guess what behaviors you are talking about or interpret vague terms such as "attitude," "defiant," "moody," etc. Descriptions of inappropriate behavior also help the youth understand your tolerance levels and limits. (See Chapter 6, "Tolerances.") Without clear, objective descriptions of inappropriate behavior, a youth may not know what behaviors are inappropriate and may continue using them.

To be most effective, such descriptions or demonstrations of behavior need to be delivered in a calm, matter-of-fact manner. Don't use a harsh or accusatory tone of voice, and don't mock the youth or exaggerate his or her behaviors. A calm approach makes it more likely that the youth will listen and learn. A belittling, harsh, or mocking approach is likely to result in an emotional reaction, and potentially, a negative confrontation.

3. Consequences

This component involves delivering negative consequences, in the form of a point loss, for inappropriate behaviors. Immediately after delivering the point fine, you should offer a positive correction statement. A positive correction statement lets the youth know that he or she will have an opportunity to immediately earn back some of the points by practicing the new skill or behavior (e.g., "You'll have a chance to earn some of those points back by practicing."). Up to half of the points lost may be earned back during the practice session. (Youth on the Achievement System earn a natural or logical consequence instead of a point fine.)

Delivering the negative consequence provides another opportunity to relabel the skill (e.g. "You've lost 2,000 points for not asking permission."). How you deliver a point fine also is important. Try to use phrases like "You've earned..." or "You need to take off...," rather than "I'm giving you a point fine..." or "I'm taking off points...." Using the first set of phrases helps the youth understand that it is his or her behavior – not yours – that has resulted in a point fine.

Youth Care Workers also should follow up with the youth later in the day to see how things are going, especially watching for the youth to use the new skill or behavior. Any use of the skill or positive behavior should be sufficiently reinforced so that the youth knows he or she did the right thing. (See Chapter 8, "Relationship-Building/ Effective Praise.")

Immediate, calm delivery of negative consequences, along with a positive correction statement, helps discourage the youth from engaging in the inappropriate behavior in the future and helps motivate him or her to learn a new skill. By not using negative consequences, Youth Care Workers may actually reinforce the inappropriate behavior with their attention, teaching, and concern. The negative consequence provides a response cost for engaging in inappropriate behavior.

4. Description/Demonstration of appropriate behavior

This component involves describing the appropriate behavior that should replace the inappropriate behavior. This gives the youth an alternative behavior. The effective use of this component is similar to Step 2 (Description/Demonstration of the inappropriate behavior). That is, it involves labeling the new skill and specifically describing the desired verbal and nonverbal behavior. Just as in describing the inappropriate behavior, you may choose to model the appropriate behaviors that make up the skill.

You can help the youth generalize the behavior or skill to other situations by explaining relevant antecedent conditions (e.g., "Whenever someone has to tell you

'No,' whether it's your parents, a teacher... here's what you should do..." or "Whenever you answer the telephone..."). Such descriptions of antecedent conditions not only help the youth generalize the skill but also offer support. Such statements make it easier for the youth to understand that the teaching will benefit him or her in many situations and is not an arbitrary process. Descriptions of appropriate behavior also should be supportive and nonjudgmental; avoid "I" statements such as "I want you to...." Phrases such as "What you should do..." or "Next time, you can try to..." sound less judgmental, yet clearly tell the youth what behaviors need to occur in the future.

Using clear skill labels along with specific, step-by-step behavioral descriptions will make your teaching more effective and pleasant, and make it more likely that a youth will successfully learn new ways of behaving.

5. Rationale

In a Teaching Interaction, a rationale is a statement that explains the benefits a youth will receive by engaging in appropriate behavior. (See Chapter 5, "Rationales.") In other words, a rationale shows the relationship between a youth's behavior and a consequence or outcome. Youth will view you as being more concerned and fair when you point out the benefits of learning a new skill or continuing to behave appropriately. Short-term, individualized rationales help youngsters internalize what they are learning and help motivate them to change. Rationales also teach morals and values and should be extended to include sensitivity to others and our relationship with God. For example, you might tell a youth, "Stealing not only causes

more problems for you, but also is wrong and hurts others."

6. Requests for acknowledgment

Requests for acknowledgment occur frequently throughout the teaching process. Checking with the youth to be sure that he or she understands what is being said lets you know that you are on the right track. These requests take the form of questions such as, "Do you understand?" or "Do you have any questions?" or "Can you repeat that back to me?"

Requesting acknowledgment is very important; it helps you promote a dialogue and avoid lecturing. It also lets you know if the youth are listening and how much they are understanding.

To effectively use this component, you need to request acknowledgment and have the youth verbally respond to the request. You also must make it clear to the youth that you are not necessarily asking if he or she agrees with what is being said, only whether he or she understands it. Avoiding questions that could spark disagreement or arguing will move the teaching process along. For example, avoid requests for acknowledgment such as, "Don't you agree?" or "How do you feel about that?" Such requests are more appropriate for counseling sessions or Daily Meeting. (See Chapter 20, "Daily Meeting and Reporting Problems.")

In addition, frequent requests for acknowledgment can provide the youth an opportunity to productively participate in the learning process.

7. Practice

During the practice portion of the Teaching Interaction, the youngster has the opportunity to actually demonstrate the skill you are teaching. This component is probably one of the most powerful and important aspects of the interaction. The practice session provides the youth with the opportunity to develop new habits and to become comfortable with new ways of behaving, before he or she has to use the new skill in a real situation.

A practice session also provides you with important information. It is really the only way you can assess the effectiveness of your teaching. Over time, you become a better teacher by closely observing the progress of youngsters during practice sessions and then making the necessary adjustments to improve your teaching skills.

Practice sessions can be most effective and most successful for the youth when they are clearly set up with specific instructions to the youth. For instance, you should clearly "set the stage" by describing the setting and antecedent conditions, and by reviewing the behaviors the youth needs to work on during the practice (e.g., "Okay, Mark, now we're going to practice how to accept criticism. I'll walk into the room..." or "When I explain that you need to set the table differently, you look at me, say 'Okay...'").

Sometimes practice sessions can be more successful if the practice situation is hypothetical but similar to the situation that triggered the Teaching Interaction. This can be particularly helpful if the original inappropriate behavior involved an emotional or intense response by the youth. In such situations, you can set up a realistic practice that involves using the new skill but not the original situation. For example, you have told a youth that he will not be able to attend a concert and he has responded by swearing and arguing. While teaching the youth how to accept a "No" answer, you would probably have the youth first practice that skill by using a pretend situation (e.g., "Joe, let's say you're going to ask me to play a video game after supper. When I say 'No,' you..."). While the situation is made up, it is nevertheless as realistic as any that the youth will experience at the shelter when asking permission to take part in an activity. After the youth successfully demonstrates the skill in the pretend situation, you should return to the original issue for a final practice and a successful resolution.

8. Feedback

Following the practice, it is important to provide enthusiastic praise and specific descriptions of appropriate behavior, and to award positive points for practicing the skill. If more corrective feedback is necessary, you can again describe the inappropriate behavior and the necessary appropriate behaviors. The youth then has the opportunity to repractice the entire skill or weak areas. The total positive points awarded for the immediate practice session or sessions should not exceed one-half of the original point loss. For example, if a youth loses 2,000 points for not following instructions, he or she can earn up to 1,000 points for practicing how to follow instructions. If multiple practice sessions are used during the Teaching Interaction, you'll need to adjust the point awards for practice accordingly so that the total positive points that are earned do not exceed half of the original point fine.

This is where you follow through on the positive correction statement you made in the third step as the youth earns back points. These points help encourage the youth because he or she has already earned back part of the point fine by engaging in the appropriate behavior.

Praise, descriptive feedback, and positive points serve to reinforce the appropriate behavior and improve the likelihood that the youth will use the behavior in the future. This type of feedback also demonstrates concern and support for the progress the child is making. As a supportive mechanism, it contributes to the positive relationship that you are developing with the youth.

9. Praise throughout the interaction

Throughout the interaction, you should remain supportive and positive by praising the youth for a wide variety of appropriate behaviors. In particular, he or she should receive brief descriptive praise for paying attention and cooperating (looking at you, answering questions, listening, etc.). Pay particular attention to positive behaviors that have been difficult for the youth in the past (e.g., listening without interrupting, accepting criticism). If a youth has had difficulty accepting point fines in the past, reinforce that skill whenever the youth is able to do so appropriately. It's also a good idea to provide a praise statement at the conclusion of the Teaching Interaction to express support and end the interaction on a positive note.

Praise throughout the interaction reinforces appropriate ongoing behaviors, again increasing the probability that such behaviors will occur in the future. Such praise also bolsters the positive relationships between you and the youth, and keeps teaching on a positive, success-oriented track.

The nine components of the Teaching Interaction can help children make tremendous gains over time. While it is necessary to master specific skills in order to effectively use a Teaching Interaction, it is much more than a technical process. Effective teaching can occur only when there is a genuine concern for the child and when there is a thoughtful, individualized approach to teaching. The interaction is like any good tool. It only works in the hands of someone who cares about his or her "craft," who has taken the time and effort to become skillful, and who knows how, when, where, and why it should be used.

▶ Special techniques and applications

An important part of being a good teacher involves selecting the appropriate teaching agenda for each youth's behavior.

In order for a youngster to learn from the teaching process, he or she must be attentive. Therefore, your first teaching priority as a Youth Care Worker is to make sure that the youth is displaying attentive behaviors, not behaviors that interfere with learning.

At Boys Town Shelters, the term "ongoing behavior" is used to refer to any inattentive or problematic behaviors that interfere with the original teaching agenda, either prior to or during teaching. As a Youth Care Worker, one of your goals should be to help the youth replace ongoing behaviors with attentive behaviors that will allow him or her to benefit from the overall teaching process. Such attentive behaviors include looking at the person who is teaching, listening without interrupting, appropriately responding to requests for acknowledgment, sitting up straight, and not engaging in behaviors such as fidgeting, sighing, etc.

A wide variety of inattentive or problematic behavior can be defined as ongoing. Such behaviors may be very overt and obvious, such as turning away, arguing, or interrupting. Or they may be more subtle, such as looking away, sighing, or mumbling. Ongoing behavior may be occurring before you even begin to teach and may occur or reoccur during the course of a Teaching Interaction, Effective Praise, or Preventive Teaching (Chapter 9).

Obviously, a youth will not learn very much if he or she is looking at the floor, mumbling, pouting, etc. Likewise, you cannot teach very well under such circumstances. In these situations, there are two basic sets of procedures that can help create a more favorable learning environment. These procedures involve either using brief, specific instructions and praise for compliance, or stopping the original teaching agenda in order to do Intensive Teaching, which is discussed in detail in Chapter 11. (We'll discuss the use of brief, specific instructions first, then give a short description of Intensive Teaching.)

Giving brief, specific instructions

When a youngster's inattentive behaviors interfere with the teaching process, one way to regain his or her attention is to pleasantly give a series of brief, specific instructions followed by praise for compliance (e.g., "Please stop sighing."). Such instructions also can be accompanied by empathy statements (e.g., "You seem a little tense. Why don't you sit down over here" or "I know it's hard to accept 'No,' but you need to look at me."). Whether or not empathy is used, the child should receive brief and sincere praise for compliance (e.g., "Thanks" or "Great, that's better!").

Giving specific instructions and praise for compliance is particularly effective when you have done a lot of Preventive Teaching and Effective Praise on instruction-following. It also tends to be more effective, like most procedures, when you intervene early, before the inappropriate behavior escalates. Pleasant, calm instructions – sometimes accompanied by empathy statements and always accompanied by praise for compliance – can frequently help the youth refocus on the task at hand. This allows you to efficiently resume the original Teaching Interaction. However, a series of harsh, demanding, or vague instructions is likely to result in a confrontation (e.g., "Stop that! Get over here! Be quiet!").

Intensive Teaching

If a youth doesn't follow your brief, specific instructions, begin dealing with his or her ongoing behavior with Intensive Teaching. In this teaching procedure, each negative behavior earns the youth a negative point consequence. The point amount of the consequences increases with each behavior or failure to comply, and the Youth Care Worker continues to deliver them until the youth stops the behaviors or until the consequences are no longer an effective motivator. When point consequences are no longer effective, the goal of the interaction is to calm the situation and guide the youth back to a point where he or she begins cooperating again.

Sometimes it will be difficult to decide whether to continue giving brief instructions or start Intensive Teaching. But if a youth is not being attentive and not following instructions, continuing to give instructions without giving consequences will not resolve the situation.

Factors that may help you in this decision include the intensity, frequency, and "intent" of the behavior. A youth who is displaying an intense emotional reaction, frequent or persistent uncooperative behaviors, or behaviors that are "intentionally" disruptive might respond best to Intensive Teaching. On the other hand, brief instructions and praise for compliance might be effective for a youth who is displaying mild inattentive behaviors that are only slightly disruptive.

The best strategy for correcting problems is to use a great deal of Preventive Teaching and Effective Praise for appropriate behaviors. (See Chapter 9, "Preventive Teaching.")

▶ Summary

"A teacher affects eternity; he can never tell where his influence stops."

Henry Adams

Frequent, direct, skillful teaching by a concerned Youth Care Worker can change not only a youth's life but the lives of everyone with whom he or she comes in contact. The effects of teaching can be far-reaching, but it will take a great effort on your part. As a Youth Care Worker, you must recognize opportunities to teach, and then teach using the methods described in this chapter. Your concern for the youth and their best interests demand teaching. A fringe benefit is that your job will become easier because there will be less confusion for the youth, less negative behavior, and greater satisfaction.

CHAPTER ELEVEN

Intensive teaching

As a Youth Care Worker, you make a tremendous investment in helping each child to successfully learn new ways of behaving. Youngsters can be remarkably responsive to your praise and teaching, and to the relationships they develop with Youth Care Workers. However, despite your best efforts, there will be times when a youth becomes unresponsive and unwilling to follow any instructions. In essence, the youth has lost self-control, and the usual teaching procedures are not working.

When a youth is a danger to himself or herself, or others, or is behaving in ways that could seriously damage relationships, or goes from being angry to being enraged, your goal must be to help the youth calm down and become attentive and responsive to the usual teaching procedures.

This is when a procedure known as Intensive Teaching becomes necessary. Intensive Teaching employs the teaching techniques that have been explained in previous chapters, but uses them in different ways and at different times to achieve the desired outcome.

The most desirable goal is to prevent the behaviors and incidents that occur when a youth loses self-control. This chapter reviews the general preventive procedures that are consistently used in the shelter to reduce the likelihood of Intensive Teaching situations. It also includes a detailed explanation of the four phases of an Intensive Teaching Interaction: the preventive phase, the crisis intervention phase, the teaching phase, and the follow-up phase.

▶ General preventive procedures

The key to dealing with behavior that occurs when a youth loses self-control is PREVENTION! Prevention begins the moment a Youth Care Worker begins working in the shelter. As you work with children, using the skills and procedures learned during Preservice Training (if you are a Boys Town Youth Care Worker) and further developed through consultation with your Staff Supervisor, you are preventing Intensive Teaching situations from occurring. Effective Praise, Preventive Teaching, Teaching Interactions, problem-solving (Chapter 19), and relationship-building all contribute to a positive atmosphere. Many times when a youth loses self-control and becomes angry, it is because Youth Care Workers have failed to use any or all of these prevention techniques.

Frequent Effective Praise strengthens appropriate behaviors and relationships. If youngsters are frequently encouraged and motivated to display appropriate behaviors, they are less likely to display inappropriate behaviors.

Preventive Teaching is one of the most important and effective ways to minimize problems. Youth Care Workers can establish expectations and supportively teach and strengthen appropriate alternative behaviors – all in the absence of inappropriate behavior. Frequent Preventive Teaching makes it more likely that youth will be able to successfully recall learned skills during difficult or stressful times. Such teaching, related to the basic curriculum skills of "Following Instructions," "Accepting a Consequence," "Accepting Criticism," and "Accepting 'No' Answers," must be done regularly to reduce the likelihood of Intensive Teaching episodes. The benefits are tremendous for the youth and for the Youth Care Workers. The only hard part about Preventive Teaching is remembering to do it!

Using Teaching Interactions to correct inappropriate behavior and to teach appropriate behavior also prevents Intensive Teaching situations. By setting clear limits, consistently teaching appropriate behavior, and intervening early to remediate inappropriate behavior, you make it more likely that youngsters will respond to your teaching rather than escalate their inappropriate behavior.

Many times, children may lose self-control and become angry simply because they are frustrated by their inability to make good decisions. Teaching children to effectively work through their problems also is an important teaching tool. (This process is discussed in detail in Chapter 19.)

Relationship-building is another key to prevention. Youth Care Workers develop relationships as they praise and teach their youth, spend time with them, advocate for them, and demonstrate their care and concern for them. In the process, each child begins to form a bond with the Youth Care Workers. This means that your opinion of the child becomes important to the child. As the relationship grows (even during the short time a youth is at a shelter), the youngster is less likely to display behavior that might "disappoint" you, and is more likely to display behavior that makes you proud. By skillfully and conscientiously implementing the Boys Town Emergency Shelter Services program every day, you can prevent situations in which the youth lose self-control and help create a stable, positive learning environment.

Intensive Teaching procedures

Concerned Youth Care Workers work hard to build on each child's strengths. However, there will be times when a youth will not respond to the usual teaching and treatment procedures. A child's unresponsiveness may involve a wide range of behaviors. The youth may be very passive, withdrawn, and silent. Or, he or she may be actively noncompliant – arguing, complaining, or swearing. Problem behaviors may even include making threats, damaging property, or becoming physically aggressive.

Despite the variety of problem behaviors, there is a common element that indicates the need for Intensive Teaching – the youth is not following instructions. Regardless of the severity or intensity of the behavior, the same basic procedures can be applied to calm the youth so that teaching can resume.

To help conceptualize the process, the Intensive Teaching procedures have been grouped into four phases: the preventive phase, the crisis intervention phase, the teaching phase, and the follow-up phase. As a youth's negative behavior continues, Youth Care Workers make a transition from one phase to the next until they've completed all the phases.

The preventive phase is designed to prevent the problem behaviors from escalating and to maintain instructional control through the use of usual teaching procedures.

If the preventive phase is ineffective, the crisis intervention phase begins. The goal of the crisis intervention phase is to calm the youth and help him or her regain self-control.

After the youth regains self-control and is again responsive and attentive, the teaching phase occurs. During the teaching phase, the Youth Care Worker continues to reinforce the youth's instruction-following skills. The Youth Care Worker then does Preventive Teaching with the youth on accepting consequences, as well as follow-up teaching on skills that would prevent future Intensive Teaching situations.

The follow-up phase refers to the period that follows the youth's loss of self-control. Here, the Youth Care Worker should consider the events surrounding the behavior and make adjustments, as needed, in the youth's target skills and Treatment Plan.

On the following pages, each of these phases and the accompanying procedures are explained in detail for an Intensive Teaching episode involving a youth on the Assessment System or the Daily Points System. An explanation of the process for a youth on the Achievement System is included later in the chapter.

Preventive phase (Phase I)

The goal of the preventive phase is to help the youth keep his or her privileges for that day by helping him or her avoid a large point fine (50,000 points). As a Youth Care Worker, you must focus on helping the youth maintain self-control and preventing the problem behaviors from continuing or escalating.

In part, Intensive Teaching episodes are preventable because the antecedent conditions that often lead to a youth's loss of self-control are fairly predictable. Frequently, the antecedent conditions involve the Youth Care Worker correcting a youth. However, remember that the youth's behavior usually is associated with a chain of possible antecedents – correcting the youth just happens to be one of them. Subsequently, the youth has difficulty accepting criticism or consequences and ultimately does not follow instructions. In addition to antecedents being predictable, it also is possible to see that a youth's inappropriate behavior is building up over time. Rarely does a youth suddenly become inexplicably "out of control." Rather, the youth engages in many behaviors that indicate a weakening of self-control (e.g., short, sharp answers; tight muscles; lack of acknowledgment).

In many cases, you will be able to get the youth to start following instructions without having the behavior escalate and without having to give a large point fine. However, it's also possible that your behavior might contribute to the youth's escalating negative behavior. Frequently, the difference between defusing a situation or creating a crisis is the skillful use of empathy, and giving the youth opportunities to recover without backing him or her into a corner.

A youth will sometimes have a series of difficult experiences (antecedents) that are not observed by the Youth Care Worker (e.g., problems at school, difficulties with friends, etc.). These problems can lead to a high level of frustration or anger for the youth, and a single interaction in the shelter or a few nor-mally routine interactions with Youth Care Workers can result in a clear, immediate loss of self-control. In such cases, the preventive phase will be very brief and you could suddenly find yourself in the middle of crisis intervention.

Since most Intensive Teaching situations can be predicted and prevented, it is important to review the procedures that can be used during the preventive phase to avoid the crisis. One general key to successfully avoiding a crisis is early intervention. At the first sign that a youth's behaviors are becoming inappropriate (e.g., harsh voice tone, not looking at the Youth Care Worker, tenseness, tight muscles, clenched jaw, etc.), the Youth Care Worker needs to intervene.

Interventions may involve Preventive Teaching or preventive prompting that is directed toward the youth's failure to follow instructions. If the youth is very tense, some important skills to preventively teach at this point would be relaxation and anger-control.

Steps for relaxation include:

- Take a deep breath.

- Tell yourself to remain calm.

- Relax tight or tense body areas.

- Visualize a relaxing scene (mountains, walking along a beach, etc.).

- Say to yourself, "One, two, three, relax."

Steps for anger control include:

- If a person is talking to you, continue listening and acknowledge what he or she is saying.

- Monitor your body's feelings and how quickly you are breathing.

- Breathe slowly and deeply.

- Tell yourself to continue breathing deeply and relax the tense areas of your body.

- If appropriate, calmly ask the other person for a few minutes to be by yourself.

- While you are alone, continue to monitor your feelings and tell yourself to relax.

(These and many other skills can be found in the Boys Town manual, *Teaching Social Skills to Youth*.)

Preventive prompting also may be effective in getting the youth back on track. Such preventive prompts involve brief, calm instructions reminding the youth of the appropriate behaviors that need to be used (e.g., "Please sit down and talk with me.").

Frequent empathy statements can be used as you preventively teach or prompt (e.g., "I know you're really upset but..." or "You must be really frustrated..."). Empathy statements are real keys to successfully preventing an Intensive Teaching situation. You need to keep in mind that this is a difficult time for the youngster. You can afford to ease up and be more empathetic in these intense situations and focus more on helping the youth retain emotional control. In particular, a series of empathy statements combined with specific instructions is frequently effective in helping the youth regain self-control (e.g., "I know it's hard to listen to criticism, but you need to sit down so we can talk about

it."). Such empathy/instruction statements also can be interspersed with reality statements (e.g., "This is not going to get you what you want," or "This is only to make things harder for you.") and reassurance statements (e.g., "I'll do whatever I can to help until this problem is solved.").

As you work with a youth, you need to be generous with specific praise and empathy when he or she does comply with an instruction (e.g., "It's not always easy to calm down, but you're doing great by choosing to sit down," or "I realize you're upset but it's great that you've calmed down and are able to listen to me."). At any point, if the youth begins to follow instructions and display important "attentive" behaviors, an Intensive Teaching situation has been prevented. Once the youth is attentive, then the original teaching agenda can resume.

At some point, you may determine that teaching, empathy, instructions, and reality statements alone are not helping the youth. When this happens, you should systematically deliver a series of point fines. The amount of time spent in providing empathy, instructions, and reality statements prior to delivering point fines depends upon the youth's behavior. For a passively noncompliant youth or a youth with mildly noncompliant behaviors, you may try these procedures longer. On the other hand, if the youth's inappropriate behavior escalates rapidly, you may deliver a point fine after only one or two attempts at empathy and instructions.

Normally, four point fines are delivered during the preventive phase. The first three fines are 2,000 negative points, 5,000 negative points, and 10,000 negative points.

Except for the point fine for the original issue, the points are given for not following instructions. They are given in increasing increments to indicate the seriousness of the situation and to help motivate the youth to behave appropriately. Each fine is followed by empathy, simple instructions, a preventive prompt about the next point fine if the youth's behavior does not change, and praise for any appropriate behavior. While specific points are not immediately awarded for these appropriate behaviors, you can indicate to the youth that he or she is beginning to earn back points for complying with your instructions. Positive points will be entered on the card only after the youth has regained self-control and has entered the point fines on the card.

If the youth begins to respond appropriately after receiving the 2,000-, 5,000-, or 10,000-point fines, no other point fines are given. A youth has the option of turning his or her behavior around at any point in the progression of negative consequences.

If the youth continues to be unresponsive after the 10,000-point fine, and persists in or escalates his or her inappropriate behavior, you should state the seriousness of the situation and give instructions in a calm but firm voice (e.g., "This is really getting serious; we have to sit down and talk."). This statement of "seriousness" serves as a preventive instruction and should only occur toward the end of the preventive phase. It is usually followed by more instructions. This gives the youth another opportunity to comply with your requests and to avoid the upcoming large fine and the loss of privileges.

The statement of the seriousness of the situation and the firm, calm instructions can be especially effective if you select and always use the same statement in such situations. The effectiveness is further enhanced if you have told the youth, through Preventive Teaching, that a large point fine of 50,000 negative points will be given after such a statement if the youth does not regain self-control and begin to follow instructions. It is imperative that you reserve such statements of seriousness for situations that warrant the 50,000-point fine.

If the firm instructions and "seriousness" statement are not effective, then deliver the fourth and final point fine – 50,000 negative points for not following instructions and losing self-control. Why deliver a 50,000-point fine if the consequences have not been effective to this point? Because it is still important, even though the youth will not write down the fine and is unlikely to change his or her behavior as a result of the fine. First, it gives you a "pool" of points to use while working with the youth since he or she can earn back up to half of the points that were lost. Second, the fine is a response cost for engaging in some fairly serious misbehaviors, and is enough to ensure that the youth won't earn his or her privileges at card conference (Chapter 17).

Because of the response cost involved in earning back privileges, the youth is motivated to learn skills that can help prevent future Intensive Teaching situations and will be less likely to present such problems in the future.

Remember, the goal of the preventive phase is to help the youth regain self-control and have him or her become attentive enough to resume the original teaching agenda. Calm, empathetic statements along with specific instructions and praise can frequently avoid a crisis and help the youth. However, if this phase is not effective, you should move to the next phase.

Crisis intervention phase (Phase II)

The goal of the crisis intervention phase is to defuse the youth's behavior and to help him or her begin to regain some self-control. During this phase, no additional point fines are given. If the youth engages in serious misbehaviors that could result in a Subsystem, this should be dealt with later. (Subsystems are discussed in detail in Chapter 16.)

A Youth Care Worker's behaviors during the crisis intervention phase are very similar to the behaviors used during the preventive phase. That is, there is a great deal of empathy coupled with specific instructions. Descrip-tions of the youth's ongoing inappropriate behavior, along with descriptions of the desired appropriate behavior, also are used to help guide the youth back to the point of following instructions (e.g., "You're walking around. Please sit down so we can talk."). As in dealing with any ongoing inappropriate behavior, instructions should first be focused on the more overt behaviors such as walking around, yelling, etc. During the process, you should continue to offer empathy and praise approximations of following instructions and other behaviors as they de-escalate (e.g., "Great, you've stopped yelling, I know it's hard to stay calm when you're upset.").

As the crisis intervention phase continues, the youth's behavior is likely to de-escalate and escalate several times. The goal is to reduce the seriousness of the youth's behavior, and bring about more frequent periods of improved behavior and compliance.

In addition to offering empathy, giving instructions, describing inappropriate behavior, and praising approximations of appropriate behavior, the following guidelines can help resolve the crisis more quickly:

- Frequently during the crisis phase, the youth will complain about how many points he or she has lost. Anytime the youth mentions points, you can respond with a variation of a positive correction statement. That is, you can offer empathy statements and indicate a willingness to help the youth earn back some of the lost points (e.g., "I know you've lost a lot of points but you'll have a chance to earn some of them back when you calm down.").

- It is important to remain calm during the interaction. Maintain an even, firm voice tone. Don't feel that you need to talk steadily or respond to every comment the youth makes; appropriate pauses also may help calm the situation. A constant stream of empathy, instructions, praise, etc., can have the same effect as "badgering" and may actually further provoke the youth.

- During the crisis, the youth may want to argue with you and thereby set up a power struggle. Avoid such confrontations by avoiding discussion of content issues. The youth may make demands (e.g., "I have the right to call my probation officer.") or accusations (e.g., "You're not fair to me."). It is very important not to be drawn into arguments or a discussion of issues. The only goal is to get the child to start following instructions and you must stay focused on that task. The best way to handle demands, accusations, arguing behavior, etc., is to offer some empathy and indicate a willingness to discuss the issue or consider the request once the youth has calmed down. Then redirect the youth back to the task at hand (e.g., "You can sure make that phone call but first you need to calm down..." or "I know you're upset and I want to talk about the fairness but right now you need to..."). By staying on task, you can avoid side issues that will only prolong the youth's inappropriate behavior and divert your attention from what you are doing.

- As you work through the crisis with a youth, it is important to stay within a reasonable distance. Stay close enough to talk with the youth but not so close that you invade the youth's "private space" and possibly provoke a physically aggressive response. If the youth is walking around the house or leaves an area, stay with the youngster but do not "stalk" him or her by following too closely. If the youngster is pacing around a room, simply stand in a strategic location or move a few feet one way or another to maintain reasonable proximity. If the youth tries to leave the shelter or go from one room to another, don't attempt to physically stop him or her by blocking an exit or grabbing the youth. However, if a youth is going to endanger himself or

herself or others, you may decide it is necessary to restrain the youngster. Anytime restraint is used, no matter how briefly or under what conditions, a Youth Care Worker should immediately call his or her Supervisor and report the incident. The importance of this procedure and additional guidelines related to youth rights are discussed in Chapter 18, "Youth Rights."

- Making reality statements, along with statements about your concern and willingness to help the youth work out the situation, also can be helpful. Reality statements are used in the preventive phase and are appropriate during crisis intervention as well (e.g., "You're not accomplishing anything this way," or "This is not helping you get what you want."). Statements of persistence and concern let the youth know that you are not going to give up and will be there to help him or her no matter how long it takes (e.g., "I really want to help you so I'm not going anywhere," or "I care about you and I'll stay with you until you calm down and are able to work on your problem."). Frequently, the youth who come to Boys Town Shelters have gotten their way or have been able to avoid dealing with their problems through unpleasant and inappropriate behavior. Therefore, it is important to let the youth know that you are not going to "go away" because of the youth's tantrum behaviors.

- Vary your own behavior, depending on the type of noncompliant behavior the youth is presenting. For example, if a youth is sullen, withdrawn, and passively defiant in his or her refusal to follow instructions, you should increase your efforts. That is, give instructions and make empathy statements more frequently, and be more assertive. If you take a passive role with a passive youth, the episode can last much longer than necessary. This can keep you from other duties you might have. On the other hand, if a youth is highly agitated and verbally aggressive, you should intersperse instructions, empathy, etc., with more periods of silence. This allows the youth to "run down," and prevents a situation in which the youth escalates his or her behavior because of your constant intervention. Remember to give a youth opportunities to relax or calm down intermittently throughout this phase.

The crisis intervention phase usually lasts about 30 minutes, but can be as short as two minutes and as long as four hours or longer. Eventually the youth winds down and begins to make some progress toward following instructions.

Teaching phase (Phase III)

This phase begins when the youth's behavior de-escalates and he or she begins to follow some instructions. In the early stages of this phase, you should continue to deliver empathy, instructions, and praise for any appropriate youth behavior.

During this process, indicate to the youth that he or she is beginning to earn back points for behavior related to following instructions (e.g., "Great, you've really

calmed down and you're doing a nice job of listening to me. You're already beginning to earn back some points."). Again, however, positive points are not specified or written on the card until the youth is able to calmly write down the negative points on his or her point card.

Prior to beginning a series of Teaching Interactions and Preventive Teaching interactions, you can determine whether a youth is ready to follow instructions by giving a series of relevant instructions and praising compliance (e.g., "Why don't you move over a little closer? Great, thanks for following that instruction. Can you look at me while we're talking? Fantastic. You're really beginning to earn some points back now."). This is a very important point. If the youth is starting to follow your instructions, but you still don't feel totally comfortable with his or her behavior (eye contact, voice tone, posture), then don't proceed. Give the youth clear explanations of your expectations, and give him or her more time to comply. It's important not to move on until you are completely comfortable with the youth's behaviors. If you do, you have, in effect, taught inappropriate behaviors and raised your tolerance level.

Once you are satisfied that the youth is calm and has regained self-control, some important Preventive Teaching occurs. Since the first task is to get the youth to accept and write down the 67,000 points (−2,000, −5,000, −10,000, and −50,000) that were lost earlier, the first teaching agenda is Preventive Teaching on how to accept consequences. After the youth practices accepting a pretend fine, have him or her write down the real fines totaling 67,000 points. Praise for continued appropriate behavior is very critical at this point, as well as awarding positive points for accepting the point fine and following instructions. These first point awards can be fairly generous (around 5,000 points each) since you need to help the youth earn back up to half the points (33,500) that were lost. Point awards for subsequent appropriate behavior can range from 1,000 to 2,500 points.

After the youth accepts the consequence, the teaching phase continues. Return to the original issue that generated the Intensive Teaching situation (e.g., accepting a "No" answer, accepting criticism, accepting a consequence) and preventively teach the appropriate skill, then re-enact the original issue. If this still seems to be difficult for the youth, tell him or her that you will wait for awhile before you talk about the original issue. But don't forget about it.

Follow-up phase (Phase IV)

After you have worked through the Intensive Teaching process, you may find yourself exhausted, emotionally drained, and maybe a little angry. Most of all, you will be relieved that the episode is over, and you can take some time to recoup and regroup. But there is one more phase to complete, a phase that is very important for the youth. After an Intensive Teaching Interaction, there are several steps you need to take in order to help the youth control his or her anger or loss of self-control in the future. This is the follow-up phase.

First, you need to look at the antecedents of the child's behavior. Was is not being able to accept a "No" answer, an upsetting phone call from mom, or a bad school day? Was it something you did or said, or was it a combination of things? Antecedents can be very complex, but by trying to relate them to specific skills (e.g., "Accepting a 'No' Answer," "Accepting Criticism," etc.), and adjusting the youth's target areas in his or her Treatment Plan accordingly, you can identify and make necessary changes.

Next, develop teaching strategies that address the adjustments to the youth's Treatment Plan. These involve Preventive Teaching with old or new skills, lots of practice, and relationship-building. You also should have the youth use problem-solving (discussed in more detail in Chapter 19) to work through difficult situations at neutral times.

Finally, be sure to reinforce appropriate alternative behaviors or the absence of inappropriate behaviors that are related to the original Intensive Teaching situation and the youth's loss of self-control.

▶ Intensive Teaching for youth on the Achievement System

Parts of the Intensive Teaching process are somewhat different for a youth who is on the Achievement System (Chapter 15).

First, logical consequences, rather than point fines, are used for youth on the Achievement System. So when an Achievement youth is involved in an Intensive Teaching situation, he or she receives logical consequences in place of the 2,000-, 5,000- and 10,000-point fines given to a Daily Points youth. (The logical consequences are taken from the Logical Consequence Menu, described in Chapter 15.)

When an Achievement youth displays ongoing behavior, a Youth Care Worker has some options available. A Youth Care Worker can, 1) do Preventive Teaching or give a preventive prompt to the youth to stop the ongoing behavior, or 2) begin Intensive Teaching. During the preventive phase, a youth first earns a logical consequence of losing one to four privileges for the original issue. (In comparison, a youth on Daily Points would lose 2,000 points.) At this point, the Achievement youth does have an opportunity to earn back the privileges.

If the ongoing behavior continues, the youth then would lose five privileges, again with a chance to earn back all or some of the privileges. (A youth on Daily Points would earn 5,000 negative points.) The next fine is a loss of all five privileges, with no chance to earn them back for 24 hours. (A youth on Daily Points would earn 10,000 negative points.) These consequences are delivered to the youth to indicate the seriousness of the situation.

At this point, the Youth Care Worker should make a statement about the situation's seriousness to the youth, and give firm, calm instructions. A youth should be pretaught that if he or she doesn't take advantage of the opportunities to earn back the five privileges, a large consequence will be given. As with the youth on Daily Points, an Achievement youth who does not comply after receiving the smaller consequences finally earns a 50,000-point fine and is placed back on a point card. The large point fine serves as a response cost

and a cushion that Youth Care Workers can use to concentrate on skills the youth needs to work on in order to prevent future episodes. No more point fines are given at this time.

When the youth has regained self-control, which should occur during the crisis intervention phase (Phase II), the Youth Care Worker begins the teaching phase (Phase III). The only point fine for the youth to write down on the point card is the 50,000 negative points. The Youth Care Worker then can begin to award the youth positive points for appropriate behaviors, just as on other Motivation Systems.

An Achievement youth whose behaviors earned a 50,000-point fine loses privileges until the 50,000 has been reduced to zero. During this time, the youth uses a point card called the Achievement Card to keep track of his or her points; even thought the youth is on a point card, he or she remains on the Achievement System. As soon as the point fine has been reduced to zero, the youth regains access to all privileges. The youth does not have to wait until card conference.

A youth who frequently engages in unresponsive behavior to the point where a 50,000-point fine is necessary may require more structure and motivation through the use of the Daily Points System. Consult a Supervisor before removing a youth from the Achievement System.

► General issues related to Intensive Teaching

The following issues and guidelines can help Youth Care Workers prevent or manage Intensive Teaching episodes:

- One aid to adjusting Intensive Teaching strategies is to chart the frequency, duration, and intensity of such episodes. This charting is particularly helpful for youth who are presenting persistent problems. Charting allows Youth Care Workers and shelter administrators to detect slight improvements that indicate that strategies are working. Often, these slight improvements would not be detected without charting, possibly causing the Youth Care Workers to discontinue or modify procedures that are in fact working. Similarly, strategies that are not working can be detected early and informed decisions affecting Treatment Plans can be made.

  Charting frequency and duration is fairly straightforward. The following scale can be used to help track intensity.

  1. Passive behavior
  2. Verbally aggressive
  3. Verbally aggressive with threats
  4. Physically aggressive to property
  5. Physically aggressive to people or animals

  Such charts also can be shared with a youth so that progress can be reinforced and discussed. A positive change in frequency, duration, or intensity is reason to praise, and improvements frequently will occur in more than one area. Youth Care Workers also can keep track of the issues and preceding conditions that lead to each Intensive Teaching episode. In this way, Youth Care Workers can do appropriate Preventive Teaching and can intervene early in the chain of behaviors to prevent a youth's loss of self-control. Remember, the key is PREVENTION!

- When an Intensive Teaching episode occurs, the Supervisor should be informed as soon as possible, even as the episode is beginning. The Supervisor probably will come to the shelter to coach new Youth Care Workers the first few times they deal with an Intensive Teaching episode.

- In order to minimize negative reinforcement a youth might receive from other youngsters, the "five-second" rule is used. This rule basically states that on a predetermined cue from the Youth Care Worker ("The five-second rule is in effect"), all other youth are to leave the area. The youth are awarded points for doing so. The rule should specify where youth should go and what they should do during the Intensive Teaching situation. This rule is not meant to punish or overly restrict the activities of the other youth. Therefore, they typically should have access to their privileges. For practical reasons, access to certain privileges or areas of the shelter may be temporarily limited because the youth who has lost self-control is in that area. Youth may earn additional points for continuing to follow instructions and for cooperation during the course of the Intensive Teaching episode. Youth Care Workers should discuss this rule during Daily

Meeting (Chapter 20) and preventively teach the procedure to the youth.

● As noted earlier, Youth Care Workers should promptly inform their Supervisor that an Intensive Teaching episode is occurring and follow any advice or other reporting procedures that are discussed. Also, if the situation seems serious, a Youth Care Worker may want to call the local police. In general, if the Youth Care Worker feels there is a serious threat of injury or is physically restraining a youth, immediately calling the local police for help is the best thing to do. In particularly difficult or lengthy episodes, the Youth Care Worker who is handling the situation may need a break; he or she can ask other Youth Care Workers or the Supervisor to take over for short periods. When assistance is used, however, it is very important that the episode be successfully concluded by the person who first began working with the youth.

▶ Summary

In summary, it is best to avoid and minimize Intensive Teaching episodes through Preventive Teaching, Effective Praise, Teaching Interactions, problem-solving, relationship-building, and by consistently using the Boys Town Emergency Shelter Services program. When such episodes occur, however, a Youth Care Worker can successfully guide a youth back to a point of self-control using the procedures discussed in this chapter. Consistently using empathy and concern, and providing opportunities for a youth to recover, also can go a long way toward quickly and effectively ending such episodes.

Overview of Boys Town shelter motivation systems

While the purpose of Boys Town's Shelters is to provide short-term care for troubled youth, efforts to teach skills and positive behaviors can have the biggest impact on shelter youth. Kids can take the alternative behaviors they learn with them, giving them a basis for building relationships and identifying options for solving problems.

But many youth who come to a shelter are not motivated to change their behavior. As we've said earlier, these youth have not learned the relationship between their behaviors and the outcomes of these behaviors. The consequences they have received in their natural environment have not motivated them enough to change their behaviors.

In these situations, an artificial means of motivation is necessary. That is why the Boys Town Motivation Systems are such an important part of the shelter teaching process.

"Without the Motivation Systems, we'd be a 'holding' facility," said one Youth Care Worker. "But we're a treatment facility and we help kids work on their problems and get better."

In many ways, a structured Motivation System is like a plaster cast used to help heal a broken leg. It is important to the healing process while it is on, and its removal is a good sign that progress is being made.

Teaching Interactions occur within the Motivation Systems. As part of the interaction, negative consequences are given for inappropriate behavior and, using the principle of positive correction, positive consequences are given to reinforce a youngster for practicing an appropriate alternative behavior. (Youngsters also can earn points for behaviors that occur outside Teaching Interactions.)

While consequences serve as the prime motivators in the behavior-change process, they are no more or less important than any of the other components of teaching. If you and other Youth Care Workers rely too much on the Motivation Systems, it may hinder a youth's development by shielding him or her from natural contingencies. Overuse also makes it a "program" focus instead of a "relationship" focus.

On the other hand, if you do not use Motivation Systems enough, your effectiveness as a teacher is reduced and the youth do not learn as quickly. Remember, consequences change behavior.

The Motivation Systems used in the Boys Town Emergency Shelter Services program are designed to help you improve and expand your personal abilities to motivate, discipline, and monitor the behavior of the youngsters in the program. But the Motivation Systems do not teach kids – you teach kids! According to one Youth Care Worker, "If we're not teaching to kids and helping them learn new behaviors, then what are we doing for them?"

Motivation Systems do not work by themselves. Ultimately, their effectiveness depends upon the cooperation of the youth and skills of the Youth Care Workers. Youth Care Workers need to use the Motivation Systems to enhance and complement their own skills and abilities as they teach the youth to become more competent adolescents, and subsequently, more successful adults. But youth should not be allowed to become dependent on the system. As they learn more skills and learn to enjoy the natural benefits of appropriate behavior, the youth

make the transition from more-restrictive Motivation Systems to less-restrictive Motivation Systems. This helps prevent overdependence on systems and prepares them for their departure from the shelter.

"Motivation is what gets you started. Habit is what keeps you going."

Jim Ryun

▶ Token economy

A token economy is a contingency arrangement where tokens are earned or lost immediately following a behavior. The tokens later can be exchanged for back-up reinforcers. There are many different types of token economies. One type is the point system used at Boys Town Shelters. Youth earn points for appropriate behavior and lose points for inappropriate behavior. Points can be exchanged for a variety of privileges that are proven reinforcers for youth. All these privileges are available within the shelter environment. Snacks, watching television, access to recreational activities, and using the telephone all are privileges available in every Boys Town Shelter program. Reinforcers available outside the shelter include outings and home visits.

The following components make up an effective token or point economy:

1. Contingency based on a point system. You might ask why we use points instead of privileges in our token economy. Why not just give and take away privileges directly? There are several advantages to using points:

- Points are always available immediately; privileges are not. So, points can be earned or lost immediately. This helps to increase the effectiveness of points as consequences.

- A youth will not get satiated on points. In other words, points will continue to motivate a youth no matter how many points he or she receives during the day. This is not the case with privileges. If a youth receives a sweet snack for every appropriate behavior, the youth would soon tire of eating snacks (satiation) and they no longer would motivate the youth to behave appropriately.

- Points, over time, actually become more powerful than any of the privileges because points represent all privileges. This eventually makes points very valuable to youth and their effectiveness increases over time.

- It is easier for Youth Care Workers to assign a proper point amount to any behavior. Subtle behaviors may earn or cost a youth only a few hundred points while significant behaviors may earn or cost thousands of points. It is difficult to break privileges down into smaller parts so they can be used as consequences for behaviors.

- The point system helps guide Youth Care Workers so they do not become too creative with negative consequences. Only privileges can be earned or lost, not basic youth rights (Chapter 18). Rights are never restricted nor are they ever earned or lost in a point system at Boys Town.

2. Daily difference. The daily difference is the difference between the number of positive points and the number of negative points a youth earns each day. For example, if a youth earns 20,000 positive points and 13,000 negative points, his or her daily difference is 7,000 positive points. A youth must earn a daily difference of at least 10,000 positive points each day to earn privileges for the next day. If the daily difference is less than 10,000 positive points, the youth does not earn privileges.

3. Card conference. Every day at a set time, a youth and a Youth Care Worker meet to discuss the youth's progress, review the youth's point card, determine if privileges were earned, and set goals for the next day based on the youth's behavior. These card conferences are a great time to build relationships with the youth and to help them learn to reflect on their current behaviors so that they can improve. (See Chapter 17.)

4. Privileges. Privileges are an important part of a token economy since a youth can exchange points for privileges. This is what motivates the youth to earn points. The following privileges are available, depending on the Motivation System the youth is on:

- **Basics** – a group of privileges that are easy to monitor and control, such as playing board games, playing basketball outside, playing in the recreation room, etc.

- **Snacks** – includes special goodies such as candy, donuts, cakes, chips, cookies, etc. Healthy snacks, such as fruit and vegetables, are provided to all youth and are not sold as a privilege.

- **Television** – includes watching entertainment shows such as situation comedies, dramas, movies, etc. News and educational programs are available to all youth and are not sold as a privilege.

- **Telephone calls** – includes calls to approved relatives or significant others whose names are on a list provided by the legal guardian. Calls to parents, guardians, an attorney, a priest, or a minister for specific purposes are available to all youth and are not sold as a privilege.

- **Free time** – unstructured time during which youth may ask to use their other privileges at their discretion.

- **Others** – includes outside shelter activities when the youth is accompanied by a legal guardian or relatives who have been approved by the legal guardian. A variety of educational and recreational activities under the direct supervision of Youth Care Workers are available to all youth each day and are not sold as a privilege.

▶ Individualized privileges

There are privileges that are available occasionally or when special circumstances arise. Access to these privileges is tailored to a child's individual needs and prices are negotiable, depending on individual circumstances. These privileges could be available to any youth on any level of the Motivation Systems, but typically are reserved for Achievement (more responsible) youth. It should be pointed out that these individual-

ized privileges are not always sold. If they are important to the development and maintenance of the relationship between you and a youth, they can be offered without any point cost. Relationship variables are never bought or sold in any Boys Town program.

Some examples of individualized privileges that can be bought by youth at the shelter are:

- **Riding in the front seat** – the privilege of riding in the front passenger seat often is sold for points to the highest bidder on any particular trip.

- **Staying up late** – youth may ask to buy a period of time that they can use to stay up past their normal bedtimes.

- **Extra phone call** – youth may buy an extra phone call to a friend.

▶ Youth rights

A right is something to which one has a reasonable claim. For example, the Constitution of the United States, the amendments to the Constitution, state laws, and court decisions that interpret all of these have specified a number of rights for all citizens. Freedom of speech, freedom from cruel and unusual punishment, freedom from unwarranted searches, etc., all are God-given human rights guaranteed to all people in the United States.

A privilege is a particular benefit that is granted to someone based on merit, position, or special decree. A privilege is something one may or may not have. A right is something one always has; it is guaranteed.

Because not all residential programs for children have respected the rights of youngsters, the courts have intervened and have begun to specify more clearly the rights of children in such programs. These "youth rights" are described in detail in Chapter 18. Here are some of the youth rights that are guaranteed for each child in a Boys Town Shelter.

1. Three meals a day.

2. A regular bed and opportunities to sleep.

3. Fresh air and light.

4. Communication with others.

5. Access to personal property.

6. Access to religious activities of his or her choice.

7. Freedom from abuse or humiliation.

8. Access to family outings, employment, and student activities.

These basic rights are not privileges and are not part of any Boys Town Motivation System.

▶ Special conditions

There are two special conditions that apply to the token economy or point system. These conditions, which are designed to help the youth be successful, are:

- **In the hole**. This refers to a situation when the total number of positive points a youth earns in one day is less than the total number of negative points. For example, during card conference, a youth adds up 10,000 positive points and 15,000 negative points. Her difference is 5,000 negative points. This youth is "in the hole," and since she did not reach the required daily difference, she will not have privileges for the next 24 hours. The negative total is not carried over to the next day. After card conference, the youth starts at zero and can begin earning points toward the next day's daily difference.

- **Zero rule**. Youth should check their point totals periodically throughout the day to determine how many they have accumulated. When a youth has more negative points than positive points, the difference is a negative number below zero. Anytime a point total falls below zero, the youth forfeits his or her privileges until he or she has earned enough positive points to get back to zero or above. This helps the youth recognize that they need to engage in more positive behaviors so they do not lose their privileges at card conference. By checking their point totals during the day, the youth have a good idea of whether they're going to have their privileges for the next day; the youth may have to forfeit their privileges for an hour or two, but they avoid losing them for 24 hours at card conference.

▶ **K**eys to effective Motivation Systems

For the Motivation Systems to provide the greatest benefit for each youngster, they must be used carefully and wisely. The following guidelines can play an important role in the effectiveness of the systems.

1. Make privileges contingent on behavior. You should use privileges as part of a Motivation System. If youth can obtain privileges without paying for them, the Motivation System becomes less effective because earning and exchanging points are no longer the only way to get privileges.

2. Individualize teaching and privileges. It is essential that you identify activities and events that are important to each youngster. These are the things that a youngster will work for and spend points on. These are the things that will motivate a youth to learn new behaviors. As you learn more about a youth, knowledge of what is important to him or her can help you tailor your teaching to maximize the benefits to that youth.

For example one Youth Care Worker was really stumped by a youth because nothing, including the usual privileges (Basics, Snack, TV, etc.), seemed to motivate him. However, when the youth casually mentioned that he enjoyed comics, the Youth Care Worker found a way to successfully motivate the youth. That Youth Care Worker helped the youngster help himself.

3. Use the Motivation Systems with the Teaching Interaction. Motivation Systems alone do not help a youngster learn new ways to behave. They work best when used in combination with interactions that help the youth learn new options in life. Teaching is the critical element; Motivation Systems only help the learning process along.

4. Teach each youth the purpose and mechanics of the Motivation Systems. You need to make sure that each youngster understands how he or she can earn and lose points, how to record the points, how to spend his or her points on privileges, and why the point system exists. It's also important to teach the youth how the point card works and to make sure they know how to use it. Your explanations will help youth learn basic connections between behavior, points, and privileges.

5. Use the principles of behavior. Use points consistently, provide points immediately, and make the size of the consequence that is earned or lost fit the behavior. The use of these principles will help reinforce and strengthen appropriate behavior, weaken inappropriate behavior, and speed up the progress of each youth. With respect to the size of a reward or consequence, it is important to remember the practice of "least restrictive alternative." This idea came out of court cases that reviewed residential treatment programs. It means that treatment providers such as Youth Care Workers should not intervene any more than necessary to accomplish a treatment purpose. So, consequences, whether they are logical or in the form of points, should be just large enough to change behavior, but should be reasonable and follow the "least restrictive alternative" concept.

Another idea related to the principles of behavior is "shaping." Shaping means reinforcing a person for using or making an effort to use at least part of a desired behavior.

For example, if you were teaching a youth good conversation skills, you might heavily reinforce him for keeping appropriate eye contact for 10 seconds and asking two reasonable questions, even though the youth had trouble completing other parts of the conversation. It's a start, an approximation to a full set of competent conversation skills. It is important to reinforce any approximation of appropriate behaviors in order to shape the youth's skills toward greater competence in life.

6. Control the systems to help achieve desired results. The Boys Town Emergency Shelter Services program represents an organized and systematic approach to solving the problems of youngsters. The procedures are there to be helpful, and for most kids most of the time, they work well. But you need to be in control of those procedures and not feel limited to just those procedures. Unique or persistent problems call for unique solutions. Youth Care Workers are encouraged to use the principles of behavior and to work with their Staff Supervisors to modify the system when necessary.

7. Focus on using positive reinforcement. As a Youth Care Worker, you should always be looking for an opportunity to "catch youngsters being good," and reinforce their appropriate behavior. This helps build positive relationships with the kids and helps to keep the focus on developing appropriate behavior. Without this, a shelter staff tends to overemphasize the negative and focus more on inappropriate behavior.

▶ **Summary**

The Motivation Systems used at Boys Town Shelters are an essential part of the teaching process. The goal is to teach youngsters the skills they need to function competently and independently in a variety of environments. Because a youth is at the shelter for only a short time, teaching focuses on referral behaviors and basic skills. As a youth learns and uses appropriate behavior more often at the shelter, in school, and in the community, the structured elements of the Motivation Systems are reduced to encourage greater independence. Eventually, a youngster must learn to maintain his or her good behavior with only the usual, natural consequences that are available to any of us; a smile, a pat on the back, a good grade, a kind word, a sign of progress, etc.

Boys Town Emergency Shelter Services Motivation Systems include the Assessment System, the Daily Points System, the Achievement System, the Makeup System, and the Subsystem. These systems are discussed in detail in Chapters 13-16.

The main point to remember about Boys Town Motivation Systems is that they are some of the best tools you have to accomplish the goal of changing a youth's behavior. When used correctly and consistently, the Motivation Systems help give structure to a youngster's life by providing the incentive to learn and use appropriate behaviors. Meshing your teaching skills with the proven effectiveness of the Motivation Systems can help provide a positive and effective program where children are happy and learning.

CHAPTER THIRTEEN

Assessment system

When a youth first enters a Boys Town Shelter, he or she is placed on the Assessment System. The youth stays on this system for three days. During this time, the Youth Care Worker who is assigned to the youngster observes the youth in order to determine his or her behavioral strengths and weaknesses.

While on the Assessment System, a youth earns positive points for appropriate behaviors and negative points for inappropriate behaviors. When a youth has a daily difference of 10,000 or more positive points, he or she can exchange them for privileges that can be used the following day.

The remainder of this chapter explains the Assessment System and its characteristics.

▶ Points and privileges

At a specified time each day – usually in the evening – each youth and a Youth Care Worker have a card conference (Chapter 17). During this meeting, the "points made" are added up, the "points lost" are added up, and the total lost is subtracted from the total made to come up with the point difference – the daily difference. On the Assessment System, if a youth has a daily difference of 10,000 or more positive points, he or she earns all the available privileges for the next day. However, if the daily difference is less than 10,000 points, the youth does not earn any of the available privileges for the next day.

The use of privileges lasts 24 hours, from one card conference to the next. So, if a youth does not have a daily difference of 10,000 or more positive points, then he or she does not receive privileges for one day, starting immediately after the conference.

In addition to determining whether a youth earns privileges, positive point differences are entered into the total-up book. (Some youth who demonstrate the ability to engage in appropriate behaviors may earn more than 10,000 points a day.) At the end of three days (the assessment period), the sum of these point totals is subtracted from the youth's System Standing, and the youth moves to the Daily Points System (Chapter 14), the next Motivation System in the shelter. The System Standing is the number of points a youth must earn in order to move to the Achievement System (Chapter 15), the shelter's least restrictive Motivation System. The System Standing is set between 100,000 and 200,000 positive points.

For example, a youth on Assessment earns a total of 10,000 positive points the first day, 10,500 positive points the second day, and 14,500 positive points the third day. If the youth's initial System Standing was set at 150,000 points, the three-day total of 35,000 points would be subtracted from 150,000. The resulting total of 115,000 points would be the youth's new System Standing as he or she begins the Daily Points System.

▶ Card conference

In addition to being a time for totaling points earned during the day, the card conference also provides an opportunity for a youth and a Youth Care Worker to discuss the youth's behaviors for that day. The youth and the Youth Care Worker complete that day's Assessment Sheet (Figure 1), discuss skills, and rate the development of the skill on a scale of one to seven, with seven being the highest rating. It is not necessary to discuss all

23 skills during a card conference, but each one should be covered at least once during the three-day assessment period. (The scale used in this system is located at the bottom of the Assessment Sheet.)

Having the youth assist in rating each skill helps Youth Care Workers build relationships with the youth and assess the youth's skill level in particular areas.

When a youth moves to the Daily Points System on his or her fourth day of placement, the skills that had the lowest average during the assessment period, along with referral behaviors, become the target skills (skills targeted for improvement) for the Daily Points System. The Assessment Sheet is no longer used.

▶ Privileges available

The Assessment System is designed to ensure the rights of each child, while making some privileges contingent upon learning appropriate behavior. (Keep in mind the differences between rights and privileges.)

The privileges a youth can earn on the Assessment System are:

1. Basics
2. Snacks
3. Television
4. Telephone calls to legal guardian and approved relatives

On the Assessment System, a youth can purchase the use of all four of these privileges for one day. The cost is 10,000 positive

Figure 1

Assessment Sheet

Name: _____

Date: _____

Skills	Specifics	Day 1	Day 2	Day 3	YCW Comments
1. Instruction following					
2. Accepts routine criticism					
3. Requesting permission					
4. Reporting whereabouts					
5. Appropriately disagreeing					
6. Rational problem-solving					
7. Expresses compliments					
8. Accepts compliments					
9. Telephone skills					
10. Greeting skills					
11. Departure skills					
12. Respects others' feelings & possessions					
13. Expresses apologies					
14. Performs daily maintenance tasks					
15. Behavior in church services					
16. Uses appropriate table manners					
17. Avoids disruptive verbal behavior					
18. Avoids disruptive physical behavior					
19. Participation in Daily Meeting					
20. Peer relations					
21. School behavior					
22. Personal Hygiene					
23. Volunteering					

Rating Scale

1 – Totally unsatisfactory	3 – Needs moderate improvement	5 – Slightly above average
2 – Needs much improvement	4 – Borderline	6 – Considerably above average
		7 – Outstanding

points. Prior to using any privilege, a youth must ask the Youth Care Worker for permission.

▶ Teaching guidelines for the Assessment System

Certain guidelines should be followed as Youth Care Workers teach youth who are on the Assessment System. First, each youth should have 25 to 35 interactions (positive and negative) recorded on his or her card each day. This is a sufficient number to ensure that effective treatment is taking place. Second, the distribution of interactions should be divided this way: 70 percent for social behaviors; 10 percent for independent-living behaviors; and 20 percent for academic behaviors. (These percentages apply to teaching that occurs during the entire time a youth is at the shelter, whether the youth is on a point card or not.) Third, Youth Care Workers should try to have eight positive interactions with a youth for every one negative interaction. This "8-to-1" ratio seems to create a good balance between positive and negative interactions. It helps ensure that the youth won't view Youth Care Workers as being too "punishing" because they do too much negative teaching, or being too tolerant of negative behavior, which can create a punishing atmosphere in the shelter. Both of these situations should be avoided.

▶ Special conditions

The conditions of both the zero rule and "in the hole," which were defined in Chapter 12, apply to point totals for youth on the Assessment System. After a card conference, the youth starts out with a new point card and a zero balance. Each day on the Assessment System is a fresh start. There is no carry over from the day before.

▶ Summary

All youth are placed on the Assessment System when they first enter a Boys Town Shelter. Youth Care Workers assess the youth's strengths and weaknesses while the youth is on Assessment, and use this information to determine treatment strategies.

While on Assessment, youth earn positive points for appropriate behaviors and negative points for inappropriate behaviors. When a youth earns a daily difference of 10,000 or more positive points in a single day, he or she can exchange the points for certain privileges that can be used during the next day. If a youth does not earn 10,000 points, no privileges can be purchased for the next day.

After a youth has been on the Assessment System for three days, he or she moves to the next Motivation System – the Daily Points System.

CHAPTER FOURTEEN

Daily points system

The Daily Points System is especially important for youth who are not motivated by verbal approval from Youth Care Workers and need more concrete rewards and punishments. Initially, this is true for nearly all of the youth who come to a Boys Town Shelter.

On the Daily Points System, a youngster earns positive points for appropriate behaviors and negative points for inappropriate behaviors throughout the day. Then, at a specified time each day, the youth and the Youth Care Workers have a card conference. At the conference, the "points made" are added up, the "points lost" are added up, and the total lost is subtracted from the total made to arrive at the daily difference. On the Daily Points System, if a youth has a daily difference of 10,000 or more positive points, he or she earns all the available privileges for the next day. However, if the daily difference is less than 10,000 positive points, the youth does not receive any of the available privileges for the next day.

Thus, a youth on the Daily Points System will either have all or none of his or her privileges on any given day. Since the use of privileges lasts for 24 hours, a youth who has a difference of 10,000 or more positive points has access to privileges immediately after the conference. A youth who hasn't earned enough points has no privileges for one day (24 hours), basically until the next card conference.

At the end of the card conference, a youth gets a new point card and begins to earn points that will count toward the next day's daily difference. Thus, a youth is earning points for the next card conference even as he or she enjoys all of the privileges that were just purchased. Usually, a youngster on the Daily Points System can earn or lose points during the card conference depending on how well he or she accepts feedback, makes optimistic statements about improving, demonstrates his or her understanding of the point system, etc.

Even when a youth does not have enough points to buy privileges during the card conference, there still is a way to earn them. Since the Youth Care Worker is in control of the point system, he or she may decide to give a youth an opportunity to earn privileges for the next day through the use of a Make-up System. (Make-up Systems are described in Chapter 16.)

▶ Privileges available

Taking into consideration the differences between rights and privileges, the Daily Points System helps to assure that youth rights are upheld for each youth while providing access to a set of privileges. This access is contingent on the youth learning appropriate behavior. The first four privileges that youth on the Daily Point System can earn are the same as those available on the Assessment System. (These privileges were discussed in Chapter 13.) A fifth privilege – Free Time – is available on Daily Points. The five privileges are:

1. Basics
2. Snacks
3. Television
4. Telephone Call
5. Free Time – unstructured time during which youth may ask to use their other privileges

On the Daily Points System, a youth can purchase the use of all five privileges for one day. The cost is 10,000 positive points. A youth must always ask a Youth Care Worker for permission before using any privileges. For example, earning the "Snacks" privilege does not entitle a youth to eat a snack anytime. The youth can ask a Youth Care Worker for a snack or accept one that is offered at snack time (usually after school or before bedtime).

▶ Teaching guidelines for the Daily Points System

The Daily Points System uses the same teaching guidelines as the Assessment System. To briefly mention them again, they are:

- 25 to 35 interactions each day
- 70 percent of interactions for social behaviors
- 10 percent of interactions for independent-living behaviors
- 20 percent of interactions for academic behaviors
- Have eight positive interactions for every one negative interaction (8-to-1 ratio)

▶ Advancement to the Achievement System

Besides earning enough points to meet his or her System Standing total, a youth must meet other criteria in order to move to the next system, the Achievement System.

First, a youth must have displayed the ability to use the basic skills that he or she has learned at the shelter. These skills include "Following Instructions," "Accepting Criticism," "Accepting "No" Answers," and "Accepting Consequences." Second, a youth must have shown improvement in referral behaviors and a willingness to set and work toward goals. Third, a youth must score 80 percent or higher on an Achievement Test. Finally, there should be a general consensus among the shelter staff that the youth is capable of moving to the Achievement System.

▶ Special conditions

The same rules regarding the zero rule and being "in the hole" that are part of the Assessment System also apply to the Daily Points System. (Both of these conditions are explained in Chapter 12, "Overview of the Boys Town Motivation Systems.")

As mentioned in the last chapter, each youth on the Daily Points System has a System Standing – the total number of points he or she must earn to move up to the Achievement System. The System Standing total a youth must meet in order to advance to the Achievement System is determined by subtracting the total number of positive points a youth earns during the three-day Assessment System from an initial point amount of between 100,000 and 200,000.

A youth's positive daily difference is subtracted from the System Standing total each day. Even if a youth earns only 5,000 positive points and cannot buy privileges, those points still are subtracted. When a youth earns more than the 10,000 positive points needed to purchase privileges each day, the extra points also are applied to the System Standing total. For example, if a youth with a System Standing of 70,000 earns a daily difference of 13,000 positive points one day, his or her System Standing would be reduced to 57,000.

If a youth on Daily Points ends the day in the hole, the negative points are neither subtracted nor added to the System Standing; in fact, they have no affect on the standing total. For example, if on Monday a youth needed to earn 40,000 more points to complete the Daily Points System, then ended up 15,000 points in the hole on Tuesday, the System Standing for Wednesday still would be 40,000. It would be a double penalty for a youth who ended a day in the hole to lose privileges for a day and have his or her System Standing increased The main effect of being in the hole is that the youth doesn't earn privileges and moves through a Motivation System more slowly.

When a youth has reduced the System Standing to zero, he or she has completed one of the criteria for advancing to the Achievement System.

▶ Summary

A youth on the Daily Points System earns positive points for appropriate behaviors and negative points for inappropriate behaviors. When a youth ends a day with 10,000 or more positive points, he or she can exchange the points for certain privileges that can be used the next day. A youth can move to the Achievement System when he or she has met the necessary criteria.

This system can be very effective in motivating youth to engage in positive behaviors and decrease or eliminate negative behaviors. However, it must be used with skill and compassion. It is not the end, only a means to an end. The next goal is to help the youth move from a somewhat artificial system to a more natural system (Achievement System) that more closely emulates the youth's home and/or community.

CHAPTER FIFTEEN

Achievement system

The Achievement System is geared for youth who have demonstrated the ability to meet all criteria set by the shelter staff in order to complete the Assessment and Daily Points Systems. It is a flexible, positive Motivation System that is based on natural and logical consequences, and social praise. (For example, if a youth shows poor sportsmanship by cheating at pool, a logical consequence might be loss of basic privileges, including playing pool, for a specific period of time.)

Just as with the Assessment and Daily Points Systems, youth on the Achievement System still are responsible for completing treatment target areas. But there are a number of differences for Achievement youth. Positive points are given only during total-up time to recognize a youth's accomplishments with treatment or target skills for the day.

Points are no longer used for immediate reinforcement because they do not reflect the type of consequences a youth will face in day-to-day situations at home, at school, in the community, etc. One of the goals of the Achievement System is to help prepare a youth for his or her next placement. Youth Care Workers must motivate youth to work toward Achievement during their shelter stay in order to help the youth have a successful transition to the next placement.

The Achievement System is the least structured of the Motivation Systems offered at the shelter. A youth on this system should demonstrate a high degree of internal motivation and should not be reliant on the immediacy of point consequences that are part of the Assessment and the Daily Points Systems.

▶ Criteria for placement on the Achievement System

A youth graduates to the Achievement System after successfully completing the Daily Points System by earning privileges at least 80 percent of the time, passing the Achievement Test (Figure 1, p. 108), and earning enough positive points to reduce his or her System Standing to zero. On the Achievement System, youth have access to daily privileges without having to earn a specific daily difference, and greater independence is expected and granted. Teaching still focuses on specific areas that need improvement and a youth's general behavior still is monitored. This is not a time for a youth's behavior to deteriorate. Rather, it is a time for the youth to learn to achieve greater independence, and to prepare to return home or move to a foster home, to independent living, or to an alternative placement.

▶ Unique features for youth on the Achievement System

The Achievement System has several unique features that are designed to help the youth obtain greater independence. One of the best features, in the eyes of the youth, is that they no longer carry a point card. The youth are given more verbal praise for completing tasks, instead of being reinforced through the token economy. Youth earn privileges without having to meet a specific daily difference, more privileges are available, and privileges can be more individualized.

The structure of the Motivation Systems is reduced but never eliminated in the Achievement System. Logical consequences from the Overall Achievement Summary (Figure 2, p. 109) are earned for appropriate or inappropriate behaviors; these are more like the consequences the youth will receive when they leave the shelter and return home or are placed in another environment. A youth has the opportunity to help determine his or her own logical consequences. This participation (the Youth Care Worker has the final decision) promotes fairness and concern. For example, a Youth Care Worker who observes a youth not accept a "No" answer appropriately might say, "Sarah, what do you think would be an appropriate consequence for not accepting my 'No' answer?" The Youth Care Worker can then use the consequence the youth suggests, choose a different consequence, or use a combination of the two.

▶ Privileges available on the Achievement System

When a youth starts out on the Achievement System, he or she has all of the privileges that were available on the Daily Points System – Basics, Snack, Telephone, Television, and Free Time. Free Time is broadened to include visits from friends, additional outings with family members, and possibly unsupervised time away from the shelter. A youth on Achievement also can negotiate for other privileges, such as special games, clothing, allowance, etc., from the Achievement Menu (Figure 3, pp. 110-111). Other privileges are available occasionally or when special circumstances arise.

▶ Teaching components within the Achievement System

Youth Care Workers interact with youth who are on the Achievement System by using Effective Praise and Teaching Interactions. Teaching ensures that the youth will continue to refine their skills. Although the Achievement System teaches youth to be less dependent on structure, it does not remove the personalized attention or education they receive in the shelter. Instead of earning positive points immediately during an Effective Praise Interaction, a youth receives social praise and/or a logical consequence.

Here's an example: A youth is on the phone with his father, and the father is swearing. The youth continues to use a calm voice and does not swear back at the father. After the phone call, the Youth Care Worker can use social praise by telling the youth, "You did an excellent job of staying calm on the phone. That helped because you didn't make the situation worse." Or, the Youth Care Worker and the youth may negotiate a logical consequence, such as an extra phone call or something from the Achievement Menu that may motivate the youth to continue the positive behavior.

If a youth engages in an inappropriate behavior, then he or she earns a logical consequence, instead of a point fine, through the Teaching Interaction. For example, a Youth Care Worker instructs a youth to clean her bedroom, including making the bed, vacuuming, dusting, and folding and putting clothes away in the right drawers. The youth does not follow the instructions completely; she does not dust her room and just throws clothes on the closet floor. Instead of earning a point fine, the youth might earn the logical consequence of completing extra chores, ones that weren't assigned prior to the inappropriate behavior.

Here are a couple of things to remember when using Effective Praise and the Teaching Interaction with youth on Achievement:

- Use least restrictive consequences.

- Use individualized consequences that are based on a youth's behaviors and referral behaviors. This means that factors like the size of a consequence or the length of time a privilege is lost or can be used may be different. For example, a youth may lose a combination of available privileges for a specific amount of time (i.e., one, three, or five hours, up to twenty-four hours).

- Make sure the choice of consequence(s) coincides with the behavior. For example, if a youth is late getting up in the morning, the consequence could be that the youth has to go to bed early that night. Here, the consequence fits the behavior.

- During the Teaching Interaction, always remember to combine the practice with an opportunity to earn back part of the consequence. For example, a youth's consequence for not getting along with another youth was loss of Basics, Free Time, and TV for five hours. If the youth practices how to get along better to the Youth Care Worker's satisfaction, the youth can earn back the use of one of those privileges in three hours instead of five. This is how positive correction is accomplished in the Achievement System. The "up-to-half-back" rule still applies as it does in point systems.

A youth who earns a consequence, whether for appropriate or inappropriate behavior, has the opportunity to help the Youth Care Worker determine the consequence using the Achievement Menu. The Individual Achievement Summary (Figure 4, p. 112) is designed to document the positive and negative consequences a particular youth earns during the day. (Each youth has his or her own sheet.) The Overall Achievement Summary is used by Youth Care Workers to document and track the consequences for all the youth on the Achievement System.

▶ Reviewing a youth's day on the Achievement System

Youth on the Achievement System review their day with a Youth Care Worker through a process that is similar to the card conference in the Assessment and Daily Points Systems. This review occurs at a specific time each day, and a youth meets individually with a Youth Care Worker to review successes and how well target areas were completed over the previous 24 hours. It is important that the youth is prepared and has all necessary review materials, such as journals, worksheets, and the Achievement Prompt Sheet (Figure 5, p. 113). The youth should do most of the talking, explaining

what he or she accomplished in target areas and the kinds of behaviors he or she demonstrated during the day to show improvement. The youth also can share concerns about negative behavior, but only for the purpose of planning how to improve the behavior and prevent it from occurring again. This teaches youth how to reflect on their day in order to help prepare for the next day.

The Youth Care Worker should use social praise and give encouragement when the youth shares information. If the youth is not sharing enough information, the Youth Care Worker may need to ask open-ended questions. This will help clarify what type of information should be shared during an Achievement card conference. Remember, the main focus should be on positive accomplishments. The Achievement card conference should be a positive, rewarding experience for the youth. When used correctly, it is a great tool for building relationships.

While a youth is discussing completion of target areas, the Youth Care Worker should stop after each one and negotiate the number of points the youth should earn for completing that particular area. (Usually, each youth has four to six target areas.) A youth can earn between zero and 500 points on the Achievement Total-Up form (Figure 6, p. 114) for each target area. The amount earned is based on effort and motivation in implementing and maintaining skills throughout the day. Allowing the youth to negotiate how many points are earned demonstrates fairness on the part of the Youth Care Worker.

When negotiations for all target areas are completed, the points earned are added up and the total is written at the bottom of the form for that day. The total also is recorded on the Achievement Savings Account form (Figure 7, p. 115), which is filled out like a checking account. If a youth chooses to "spend" some of his or her savings for a special privilege, the amount spent is deducted from the total savings amount. Points a youth earns cannot be taken away as a consequence. However, youth who do not have privileges may not be allowed to spend the points they have until privileges are earned back.

If a youth consistently fails to complete target areas or has little or no input about events related to the target areas for the day, he or she can lose privileges as a consequence. Also, if a youth does not complete a target area, he or she may not negotiate for any points, and the total for that target area is zero. Negative points are not earned on the Achievement System. The youth also needs to set both short- and long-term goals to enhance participation and to be prepared for the next Achievement card conference.

▶ Achievement System benefits for Youth Care Workers

The Achievement System can be a fun, motivational tool for Youth Care Workers as they work with youth in the shelter. It allows greater creativity in designing special privileges and independence-oriented treatment goals. Using logical consequences for appropriate and inappropriate behaviors enables Youth Care Workers to be consistent and helps assure fairness to the youth.

The Achievement System has other benefits. It allows the Youth Care Worker to continue to monitor basic skills and subtle social behaviors. It helps the youth make a smoother transition to their home or next placement. It promotes concern and fairness by having the youth participate in choosing their own consequences.

The Achievement System also allows the Youth Care Worker and the youth to target problem behavior areas while maintaining control of other appropriate behaviors. Youth Care Workers still use Effective Praise and Teaching Interactions immediately after behaviors that occur throughout the day.

▶ Summary

When used appropriately, the Achievement System is effective and can be fun for the youth and the Youth Care Worker. It is the Youth Care Workers' responsibility to motivate youth to reach the Achievement System. Remember, the Achievement System reflects an environment that is similar to that which the youth will experience when they leave the program, and is designed to prepare them for that environment.

Figure 1

Achievement Test

1. What are the five privileges you earn when you have your privileges?

2. If Tricia's mom told Tricia to make her bed, how should she follow her mom's instruction?

3. List the three Motivation Systems in order.

4. If the fire alarm goes off, where should Michelle meet everyone?

5. If your mom says to you, "You aren't wearing that ugly thing; it doesn't match," how should you accept the criticism?

6. Eric asked his dad if he could go over to Chuck's house for awhile and his dad said "No." How should Eric accept the "No" answer?

7. List your target areas and explain why you have these.

8. What should Hope do when the staff calls the "five-second rule?" Why is this important?

9. List three Basic privileges.

10. If you wanted to use something that belongs to someone else, what should you do?:
    a. Just use it   b. Ask permission   c. Forget about it

11. If you know someone who has drugs or weapons, or is thinking about running away, what should you do?

    a. Report the problem to a staff member   b. Don't say anything   c. Ignore the situation

12. List two ways you've improved since coming to the shelter.

13. List one goal you will try to work on at the shelter.

14. Use the **SODAS** method to problem-solve this situation: "Some kids are making fun of me."

15. Jim comes home to find his parents intoxicated and yelling and hitting each other. Pick three options Jim could use.

Ask for help	Go to his room	Yell and scream
Try to stop the fight	Leave the house	

Figure 2

Overall Achievement Summary
(Logical Consequence Menu)

Date: _2/1/97_

Youth	Basics	Snacks	TV	Phone	Free Time	Extra Job/ Volunteer	Bedtime	Study	Other
Jim	None til 5pm		None til 5pm		None til 5pm				
Sara		One can pop						1/2 hour extra study	
Tiffany	None til 3pm								
Anthony	←	None til 3pm			→				

For the OTHER category, refer to the list of logical consequences that is provided.

Figure 3

Achievement Menu

ITEM	COST
Additional can of pop	1000
Candy or snack	1000
Staying up late:	
15 minutes	1000
30 minutes	2000
Friend visit	5000
Movie rental	4000
Video game (Nintendo® – twice weekly)	3000
Off campus: Mall shopping, movies, skating, arcade, miniature golf	10000
Personal hygiene items (Chapstick®, shampoo, conditioner, nail files)	1000
Buy out from "Constant" chore for day	4000
Buy out from "Major" chore	7500
Buy out of study time:	
15 minutes	1000
30 minutes	2000
1 hour	4000
Additional telephone time (five minutes on local call)	1000
Additional local phone call (10 minutes)	2000
Additional long-distance phone call (10 minutes)	4000
Change bedrooms (must be okayed by supervisor)	10000
Order a pizza (arrange one day prior)	10000
Buy a book or magazine	1000-3000

ITEM	COST
Grab bag (if available)	3000
Buy a plant	4000
*Sports or school event	5000
Walkman® – one hour	2000
Money – for outings or prearranged items (per dollar)	2000
*Taking a walk	2000
TCBY®, Dairy Queen®, Daylight Donuts®	5000
Fast food restaurant with staff	8000
Paint a T-shirt	5000
Shop in Achievement closet (cost negotiable)	1000-10000
Special meal deal (plan a meal for shelter)	4000
Puzzles	3000
Models – cars, airplanes	5000
Trading cards (50)	1000
Portable radio (can be used in rec room, outside during free time)	3000
Write letter to a friend (check restrictions)	3000
Sit in living room during study time for 30 minutes	2000
You name it (points negotiable)	

*Special arrangements needed

Individual Achievement Summary
(Logical Consequence Menu)

Figure 4

Youth: _John Smith_

1. Basics
2. Snack
3. Television

4. Telephone
5. Free Time
6. Extra Job/Volunteer

7. Bedtime
8. Study Time
9. Other

DATE	Privileges	Amount	Curriculum Skill	Specific Behavior	YCW	SK	TS	+ -	YCW
2/1	1,3,5	Till 5pm	Getting along with others	Raising voice	3	1	1	0	TF
2/2	8	1/2 hour extra study time	School behavior	Being off task	2	3	2	0	AM
2/2	4	One 10-minute phone call	Staying calm	Didn't raise voice on phone	1	1	1	1	RP

For the OTHER category, refer to the list of logical consequences that is provided.

Figure 5

Achievement Prompt Sheet

DATE: _____*2/1*_____

JOBS	YCW:		VOLUNTEERS	YCW:
1. *Took out garbage*	*MR*		1. *Helped Tiffany set table*	*MW*
2.			2.	
3.			3.	
4.			4.	
5.			5.	

CONVERSATIONS	YCW:		COMPLIMENTS	YCW:
1. *Talked to Sara about sports*	*RP*		1. *Told Jim he did a good job with his art project*	*TR*
2.			2.	
3.			3.	
4.			4.	
5.			5.	

Figure 6

Achievement Total-Up

Youth Name: _____ *John Smith* _____

DATES	2/1	2/2				
TARGET AREAS						
Getting Along with Others: * 2 positive conversations * 2 volunteers	200	300				
School Behavior: * Complete and turn in homework daily * Be to class on time	425	300				
Self-Esteem: * Read 10 pgs in self-esteem book and take notes * List 2 positive things about yourself	350	425				
Staying Calm: * Ask for time when upset * Role-play staying calm daily	275	350				
DAILY TOTAL	1250	1375				

Figure 7

Achievement Savings Account

Youth Name: _John Smith_

Date	Points Deposited/Explain	Points Withdrawn/Explain	Balance Forward
2/1	1,250/Total-up		1,250
2/2	1,375/Total-up		2,625
2/2		1,000/Can of Pop	1,625

Make-up systems and subsystems

Most of the time, the regular Motivation Systems used in the shelters are sufficient for dealing with the positive and negative behaviors of youth residents. At times, however, Youth Care Workers encounter situations in which a youth's behavior warrants special measures. The Make-up System and Subsystem, variations of the shelter Motivation Systems that have already been discussed, are two such measures.

The Make-up System provides youngsters with the opportunity to earn back lost or unearned privileges between card conferences. This helps to keep each youth motivated and working for privileges. However, the use of Make-up Systems is not automatic. A youth can ask to be placed on Make-up, or a Youth Care Worker can offer it to a youth who has not earned his or her privileges. It is the Youth Care Workers' decision; as always,

they are in control of the system and must exercise good judgment.

A Subsystem is a highly structured teaching system that is used when a youth is involved in serious negative behavior. Such behavior would include stealing, using drugs or alcohol, running away, police involvement, aggression, and so on.

Basically, a Subsystem is like the Daily Points System except a youth must earn a higher number of points in order to buy fewer privileges. Here, 20,000 positive points are required for Basics, Snacks, Television, and one approved five-minute telephone call. Except under unusual circumstances, Free Time away from the Youth Care Workers is not available.

While a youth on a Subsystem must work harder to earn points, and has access to fewer privileges, the intent is not to punish.

The main reason for using a Subsystem is treatment.

When a youngster is having serious problems, it makes sense to increase the amount of time the youngster and the Youth Care Workers spend together. Because a Subsystem requires a youngster to earn extra points each day, Youth Care Workers have more points to use as positive consequences in the treatment of the youth's major problem. This means the youngster will be interacting with the Youth Care Workers more and going out of the shelter less. This allows the Youth Care Workers to work intensively with the youth to teach alternatives to the serious problem behavior.

The remainder of this chapter will explain the Make-up System and Subsystem, and their roles in the treatment provided by the shelters.

▶ Make-up System

The general ideas behind the Make-up System are these:

- There should always be a way for a youngster to earn privileges, either by meeting the requirements of one of the regular Motivation Systems or, with the Youth Care Worker's permission, by meeting the special requirements of a Make-up System.

- Meeting the regular requirements of one of the Motivation Systems is always the easiest way to earn privileges. Make-up Systems always require about twice as much effort for the same privileges.

- Earning privileges through the Make-up Systems never results in extra benefits for a youth. The extra points that must be earned under a Make-up System do not apply to a youth's System Standing or other privileges. The extra points are used only for the privileges that are being made up.

These general ideas are applied differently in each of the point systems.

This is how the Make-up System works:

If a youngster on the Assessment System (Chapter 13) or the Daily Points System (Chapter 14) fails to earn 10,000 points on a Monday, he or she has no privileges on Tuesday. However, if during the Monday evening card conference the Youth Care Worker agrees to put the youngster on the Make-up System, the youth can immediately begin earning points for Tuesday privileges and earn those privileges back before the next card conference.

The youngster is required to earn double the normal daily difference (20,000 positive points) to buy back his or her privileges. When that 20,000-point total is reached, the youth writes "make-up" in the "Curriculum Skill" column and writes 10,000 in the "Negative Points" column of his or her point card. These points are used to purchase the privileges, and the youth has access to all the privileges available on his or her Motivation System immediately. The 20,000-point requirement also helps to ensure that the youngster will have enough points to purchase privileges for Wednesday. That is, after the youth has paid 10,000 for the make-up privileges, he or she still has a balance of

10,000 points on the card, which means that he or she has enough points to earn privileges at the next card conference on Wednesday. These are "regular points" that apply to privileges, System Standing, etc.

In this way, a youngster who falls behind on points can, through some extra effort, catch up and enjoy privileges.

(There is no Make-up System for youth on the Achievement System because of the way the Achievement System is structured.)

▶ Subsystems

Before placing any youth on a Subsystem, Youth Care Workers must first receive permission from their Supervisor. Consultation in this area is important because if the behavior is serious enough to warrant a Subsystem, a good treatment strategy must be developed in order to correct it and teach alternative positive behaviors.

Youth Care Workers must answer a number of questions when the decision is made to use a Subsystem: What was the problem behavior? What kind of teaching needs to be done? What are the appropriate, alternative behaviors that need to be taught as part of the Treatment Plan for this problem behavior? How much time will be needed to practice all these new behaviors with the youth?

Youth Care Workers must remember that the Subsystem plan must be therapeutic in nature, not punishing. A revised Treatment Plan is established during the Subsystem and continues after the youth has completed the Subsystem.

There are two types of Subsystems: Straight Fine and Time-Based.

▶ Straight Fine

The Straight Fine system is used most often at Boys Town Shelters. When a youth is placed on a Straight Fine Subsystem, he or she is removed from the regular Motivation System. A youth on the Daily Points System would lose or forfeit the points earned that day, but the System Standing would not be affected. A youth on the Achievement System would not earn any points that day but would not lose Point Savings that had been accumulated. (Under most circumstances, youngsters return to the system they were on once they have completed the Subsystem.)

A point total for the Straight Fine Subsystem must be established. This is the number of points a youth must earn in order to be taken off the Subsystem and returned to his or her original Motivation System. To set this up, and keep track of the conditions of the Subsystem and the youth's progress as he or she accumulates points, the Subsystem Worksheet is used (Figures 1 and 1a).

It is important to remember that youth are in the shelter for only a short time. Because it would be difficult for a youth to earn a large number of points in order to be taken off a Subsystem before leaving the shelter, Youth Care Workers should avoid setting point totals that are too high. Again, careful consultation with the Supervisor is necessary before a youth is placed on a Subsystem. Reasonable amounts would range from 50,000 to 200,000.

Figure 1

Subsystem Worksheet

Youth: _____ Date: _____

Behavior Necessitating Subsystem: _____

Specific Description of Behaviors Necessitating Subsystem	Points	
Total Negative Points		
Specific Description of Appropriate Behaviors	Points	
Total Positive Points		

Type of Subsystem to be used _____

Privileges available on Subsystem _____

Days on Subsystem _____ Multiplied by Daily Difference _____ = Net Subsystem _____

Skills to teach:

Evaluation of Subsystem		
# of Days privileges earned:	Total # of points earned on Subsystem	
	Positive	Negative

Comments:

Figure 1a

Planned Teaching:	Spontaneous Teaching:
Motivation Systems:	Relationship Development:
Self-Government:	Counseling:
Other:	Follow-up:

Initial and Date					
YCW	YCW	YCW	Supervisor	Youth	

This is how the Straight Fine Subsystem works:

While on the Subsystem, a youth's daily difference requirement for privileges is doubled to 20,000 points. Those points can buy only the privileges of Basics, Snacks, Television, and one approved five-minute telephone call. Free Time is not available.

The points the youth earns each day are subtracted from the total remaining on the system until the entire Subsystem fine is reduced to zero. About half the points needed each day are earned in the same way that all youngsters earn points. It is just part of the daily routine. The youth earns the other points that are needed each day by working with the Youth Care Worker on the Treatment Plan designed for the youngster's area(s) of difficulty.

Time-Based

This system usually is used when a youth is near the end of his or her stay at the shelter. The purpose of doing this is to create a situation where youth can leave the shelter on a positive note, if possible. Since it's difficult to determine how long it might take a youth to complete a Straight Fine Subsystem, a Youth Care Worker can put the youth on a Time-Based Subsystem (a system based on time rather than on a point total) for the remaining days of his or her stay. This allows youth to complete a Subsystem and leave without feeling bad because they had not earned back the required amount of points.

A youth on a Time-Based Subsystem is removed from his or her Motivation System. The Youth Care Worker determines the length of the Subsystem by considering the youth's behavior and the number of days he or she has left at the shelter. This Subsystem should last from one to five days, and the youth stays on it the entire period, regardless of whether or not he or she earns privileges. For example, a youth who is put on a three-day Time-Based system at 4 p.m. Monday must stay on the system until 4 p.m. Thursday.

The youth's daily difference is still 20,000 points. Privileges available for reaching that goal are the same as for Straight Fine – Basics, Snacks, Television, and one approved five-minute phone call.

▶ Treatment Plans for Subsystems

When a youngster is placed on any Subsystem, Youth Care Workers need to have a clear idea of the behaviors they will reward with positive points or try to discourage with negative points. It will be this part of the Treatment Plan that helps the youngster overcome his or her serious problem.

Usually, the Youth Care Workers and the Supervisor work out a Treatment Plan and go over it with the youth. The youth should understand the conditions of the plan, how it will be carried out, and approximately how long he or she will be on this system. This gives the youth hope because he or she knows that the system will have an ending.

An example of a Treatment Plan for a Subsystem for drug use is provided in Figures 2 and 2a (pages 124 and 125). The plan should provide an idea of the concepts that are taught and the kinds of behaviors that will earn positive or negative points during a particular Subsystem.

▶ Factors to consider

There are some general issues regarding Subsystems that need to be considered. Of course, the basic consideration is whether or not to put a youngster on a Subsystem. Here, Youth Care Workers need to think not only about the severity of the behavior but also about the youth's stage of development. Has the youth developed a relationship with the Youth Care Workers and other shelter youth? Is he or she upset and embarrassed about the behavior problem?

These emotional changes are very important factors. Trying to bring about positive changes in behavior and relationships is the goal of using the Motivation Systems. If a youngster is appropriately apologetic, remorseful, and contrite, then a Subsystem may not be necessary in some situations. Basically, the Motivation Systems are necessary to teach basic skills, provide some structure, and build relationships. Relationships have to continue to develop as Youth Care Workers work to move each youth toward the least restrictive Motivation System.

However, if a youth is placed on a Subsystem, the following general guidelines should be considered:

- **Don't make it too hard to earn points**. The youngster must earn more points to pay for fewer privileges. Keep the Treatment Plan in mind and deliver points for positive behaviors you might otherwise overlook. The idea is not to punish, but to teach.

- **Do not be afraid to let a youngster earn his or her privileges**. There are fewer privileges available anyway, and Basics, Snacks, Television, and one telephone call a day are the minimum privileges each youngster should have if he or she is trying. If a youngster on a Subsystem goes two days in a row without earning privileges, pay special attention and have him or her stay close by so that there are plenty of opportunities for the youth to earn points on the third day. This will help him or her make the daily difference requirement and earn the privileges.

- **Give lots of points for an "I-can-do-it" attitude**. Reward effort, cooperation, and remorse. If a youth on Subsystem does not earn privileges and you are having a hard time motivating him or her, talk to other Youth Care Workers and the Supervisor.

- **Increase the frequency of "personalized counseling" during a Subsystem**. Because a Subsystem is restrictive, it is important for you to show care and concern for the well-being of the child.

- **Expect the youngster to be somewhat depressed**. Given what he or she has just done and the restrictive nature of the Subsystem, the youngster should be a little down. You should be understanding and always have some high-paying rewards for positive behaviors available so that there is a "light at the end of the tunnel."

- **Do not make up your own punishments**. You don't need to be socially punitive or dream up dirty jobs that need to be done. You may be very angry, upset, or disappointed in the youth, but remember that you are a

Figure 2

Subsystem Worksheet

Youth: _John Smith_   Date: _2/1/97_

Behavior Necessitating Subsystem: _Using Drugs_

Specific Description of Behaviors Necessitating Subsystem	Points	
Smoking marijuana	50,000	
Giving marijuana to peers	50,000	
Dishonesty when asked about drugs	50,000	195,000
Phone call from the principal	20,000	
Unexcused absence from algebra	25,000	
Total Negative Points		
Specific Description of Appropriate Behaviors	**Points**	
Turning in the drugs	25,000	
Self-reporting	15,000	
Apology to the principal	15,000	75,000
Apology to the algebra teacher	10,000	
Honesty about sharing the drug with peers	10,000	
Total Positive Points		

Type of Subsystem to be used _Straight Fine Sub_

Privileges available on Subsystem _Basics, Snacks, TV, One approved 5-minute phone call_

\# Days on Subsystem _6_ Multiplied by Daily Difference _20,000_ = Net Subsystem _120,000_

Skills to teach: Saying "No" to peers   Honesty

               Reporting whereabouts   The danger of drugs

Evaluation of Subsystem		
# of Days privileges earned:	Total # of points earned on Subsystem	
	Positive	Negative
Comments:		

Figure 2a

Planned Teaching:	Spontaneous Teaching:
Each day: 1. Role-play 3X "Saying 'No' to drugs." 2. Role-play 2X "Honesty." 3. Role-play 2X "Reporting whereabouts."	1. Reinforce youth for engaging in positive activities with his peers. 2. Reinforce the youth for not using drugs. 3. Reinforce the youth for staying in each class, having no tardies, and having his school card signed.
Motivation Systems: Each role-play 1,000 - 2,000 Counseling sessions 2,000 - 5,000 Drug Reports 10,000 - 20,000 Not using drugs 15,000 each day Presenting in Daily Meetings 10,000	**Relationship Development:** 1. Encourage youth to engage in *positive* activities with peers. 2. Encourage the youth to be involved in family and extracurricular activities.
Self-Government: 1. Discuss in a group how you can tell a peer "No" to drugs. 2. Have the youth present his three papers on drugs. 3. Have the youth vote on whether the youth used drugs that day.	**Counseling:** 1. Discuss with youth the dangers of using drugs. 2. Talk to youth about how to select appropriate friends. 3. Explain to youth the legal risks of using drugs.
Other: Have youth research drug information and write three, one-page reports. 1. The dangers of marijuana. 2. How drugs can affect other parts of my life. 3. How can you use drugs in an appropriate way?	**Follow-up:**

Initial and Date					
YCW	YCW	YCW	Supervisor	Youth	

teacher and a role model. The Subsystem is difficult enough; you can let it do its job while remaining positive and empathetic.

- **Subsystem points apply only to reducing the Subsystem total and do not affect regular system totals.**

- **During his or her time on a Subsystem, include the youngster in group outings, shelter events, and normal interactions.** Quality of life for the youngster does not have to be diminished in order for the Subsystem to be effective. However, you should spend more time monitoring and being with the youth.

- **Do not expect immediate changes in the youth's behavior just because a Subsystem has been implemented.** These youngsters have real problems. Real solutions may take a little time. Remember to hang in there and keep teaching to help the youngster solve his or her problems.

- **Get the Supervisor's permission before placing a youngster on a Subsystem.** Don't hesitate to consult with the Supervisor if problems arise.

▶ Summary

Like all Motivation Systems, Make-up Systems and Subsystems are designed to help children learn appropriate behaviors and correct inappropriate behaviors. Since they are specialized teaching methods, it is essential that Youth Care Workers understand how they are used and how to achieve the best results.

Make-up Systems give a youth an opportunity to earn privileges, even when he or she has not been able to accumulate enough points during the course of the day. This gives a youngster hope, no matter how badly the day has gone.

Subsystems allow Youth Care Workers to work more closely with a youth who has broken the rules so that the youth can learn from his or her mistake. The Treatment Plan developed for a youngster on a Subsystem is a cooperative effort by Youth Care Workers and their Supervisors. The goal of the plan is not to punish, but to teach.

CHAPTER SEVENTEEN

Card conference

Card conference is not a time of judgment. However, it is a time when youth are, in a sense, held accountable for the choices they made during the previous 24 hours.

Card conference is a time set aside every day for each youth to meet with a Youth Care Worker to review the youth's day. They also plan for the next day and discuss any concerns the youth might have.

Youth who are on point cards total up their points and exchange them for privileges. Achievement youth talk about their day, review target areas, and negotiate for points.

"We judge ourselves by what we feel capable of doing; others judge us by what we have done."

H.W. Longfellow

▶ Guidelines for card conference

Card conference takes place seven days a week, except for certain times like holidays when the youth might be given a "system vacation." A conference usually lasts from five to twenty minutes, and is scheduled for the same time each day. For example, if you set 4 p.m. as card conference time, all the youth need to have their target areas (specific areas of focus) completed by that time. You may not total up all the youth precisely at 4 p.m., but this provides a deadline for the youth to meet.

During a conference, you should focus on a youth's accomplishments, praising and encouraging the positive choices he or she has made. Even if a youth had a particularly negative day, your focus should be on the positive events and what the youth can do differently to make the next day better. Special attention should be given if a youth accomplished particular goals.

Since this time is set aside specifically for one-on-one discussions between a youth and a Youth Care Worker, it is important that Youth Care Workers give youngsters their undivided attention. The shelter can get busy, and it is sometimes difficult to give youth individual attention, so you must take advantage of this "built-in" time. Being alone also allows youth to discuss sensitive topics they might otherwise not want to talk about with other youth around.

Card conference is a great time to "set the youth up for success," or proactively teach. One way to do this is to introduce and consistently use goal-setting. Most youth who come to a shelter don't know what goal-setting is or how to do it, so an explanation usually is necessary. But once they understand the idea, they should be able to set and achieve goals on their own. It's important here to start with small, short-term goals; that makes it easier for you and other Youth Care Workers to determine whether or not the youth are accomplishing the goals they set. Even more importantly, the youth have a better chance of achieving small goals, and this can give them confidence and a sense of accomplishment. Possible goals for a youth might be making a phone call to apologize to a parent, talking with a parent in a calm voice tone, or getting an "A" on a test or quiz. Youth also may set a goal of having no more than one negative consequence for anger control on the next day's card. Youth Care Workers need to guide this process, and get the youth excited about setting goals.

Finally, you should teach youth how to present themselves and their day. Teaching social skills is an extremely important part of your job and this social interaction can reap positive results. The youth should be attentive, sitting up straight, looking at you, and acknowledging your conversation. They also should be assertive, and be their own public relations persons. Their future – the next 24 hours – is at stake, and they need to advocate for themselves. Teaching and practicing this will help them see the cause-and-effect relationship between their behaviors and what happens to them, and may give them the spark they need to believe that they can choose and control their destiny rather than just reacting to what goes on around them. This doesn't mean that bad choices they've made are forgotten; rather, it helps youth recognize their good choices, and teaches them how to present themselves well and be genuinely excited. If they have made bad choices and won't earn privileges, they can admit to their error and confidently set out to change what they can control – the choices the youth will face until the next card conference.

▶ Steps to card conference

The first matter of business during card conference is having the youth total up his or her point card. Sometimes, a youth will do this before the meeting, and that's fine. Either way, the youth needs to do the math, which helps sharpen his or her math skills.

When the youth is finished totaling up, you should verify the point totals and generally look over the whole card. Pay close attention to specific areas, such as whether the youth has completed target areas and whether he or she has added unearned points or otherwise manipulated the point amounts on the card. You also should check the overall appearance of the card for spelling and hand-writing. Youth who are on Achievement need to begin presenting their day during this time by reviewing their target areas and discussing how they may have applied them.

Above all, look for things to praise. When youth complete their target areas, praise them for it. If they returned from a suc-cessful home visit with their parents or had a good day at school, then focus on these areas. However, if a youth has had a bad day, briefly mention specific problems, then discuss the youth's improvements, or set some goals, again emphasizing the positive.

During card conference, some youth may not earn their privileges. In these situa-tions, it's important to do Preteaching about this issue, reminding the youth about anger control, accepting "No" answers, and accept-ing decisions of authorities. Youth are often disappointed in these situations, but matters will only get worse if they don't accept not having earned their privileges.

For youth who are on a point card, a Youth Care Worker should write the total from their cards in the total-up book. Youth should then fill out a new card, including the next day's date, target areas, and their new System Standing. Before a youth leaves the meeting, he or she should earn points – usually 500 to 1,000 – for following the instruction of filling out the point card. Youth also can earn points for setting a goal or improving their self-esteem. This gets the youth started on the next 24-hour period with a positive point balance.

After the conference, Achievement youth enter their points in their Achievement Savings Account. A Youth Care Worker should check math and point totals here also. The youth may ask to purchase something with their points at this time.

The end of the meeting is a good time to discuss the youth's understanding of the shelter's Motivation Systems. You can ask them about the next system and discuss how important it is to reach it, as a way of moti-vating the youth to work toward it.

▶ Tips for card conference

If a youth hasn't earned enough points to get his or her privileges, don't give points away or award points just to make sure the youth gets them. This will send a confusing message, and the youth may think that they will always get privileges, even if they don't earn the required number of points. Card conference also is a good time to place a youth on a Make-up System or Subsystem, if the situation warrants.

▶ Summary

Card conference should be a benefi-cial time for the youth. It provides an oppor-tunity for a Youth Care Worker and a youth to spend time together. If you follow the guide-lines (e.g., praise, encouragement, setting goals, etc.) and use the steps (e.g., emphasiz-ing the positives, mentioning the negatives, etc.), this meeting can be the highlight of a youth's day, as well as a chance to check his or her compass and change directions in behav-ior, if necessary.

Youth rights

As child-care facilities, Boys Town Shelters assume considerable responsibility for the youngsters in their care. In a sense, staff members become the parents, teachers, and protectors for each youngster. In these roles, staff have considerable authority as they guide and oversee nearly every aspect of each youth's life while the youth live in the shelter.

While they have considerable authority, it is not unbounded authority. For example, Boys Town Shelter staff take on the responsibilities of a parent and act in the place of the parent, but do not have all the rights and options of a parent. Parents can do many things for, with, and to their own children that are legally, morally, or ethically beyond the reach of any other person or agency such as Boys Town. Yet, Boys Town still must successfully carry out many duties and responsibilities for the children in its shelters. Thus, in its role *in loco parentis* (in the place of parents), Boys Town must serve the best interests of each youngster in every way.

Organizations that care for children have always had the duty to responsibly act in place of parents in order to serve the best interests of each child. Sometimes this has not been the case. Too often, abusive practices have been used to maintain order or to ease the burdens of operating a program. Too often, the individual child was not served well.

Public exposure of these abuses in the 1960s and 1970s led to changes, however. Organizations were sued, state and federal regulations were issued, legislative bodies passed new laws, new licensing and regulatory requirements were adopted, and new professional standards were defined and implemented.

All of this activity was designed to ensure that each agency would indeed act in the best interests of each child. Children came to be seen as having rights. But because the first court case involving children's rights wasn't until the 1960s, there still is a considerable lack of clarity about the rights of children in residential care. Some legal interpretations of children's rights are very expansive, while some residential practices are very restrictive.

Boys Town has examined these issues and developed a comprehensive system that aims to maximize the freedom of children, prevent their abuse, and foster humane, effective care. Our mandate is, "As much freedom as possible; as little restriction as necessary."

Boys Town is committed to providing a safe environment for each and every child served. A safe environment not only is free of abuse, but is one in which a child can grow spiritually, emotionally, intellectually, and physically. It is an environment that respects the rights of a child and employs the most positive practices in caring for children.

▶ **Youth rights components**

The Boys Town approach to promoting safe environments has multiple components. They are:

- Policies and procedures
- Training in positive interaction styles
- Ongoing program evaluation
- Regular youth interviews
- Feedback from outside consumers
- Staff Practice Inquiries
- Training in the rights of children

All of these components are integrated into a system of child care where the main provision is safe, humane care. Information gathered through the use of these various components is constantly used to update and modify the program as it becomes necessary.

Policies and procedures

The commitment of the Boys Town's Emergency Shelter Services program to provide safe environments begins here. Each staff member is made aware of written policies and procedures that relate to protecting the rights of children. These not only emphasize the intent of the program, but also spell out the procedures that are followed when possible policy violations occur. Policies and procedures set in motion other specific components.

Training in positive interaction styles

All staff are trained in how to interact positively with children and how to help them change their behavior while respecting their basic dignity and freedom. (See Chapter 10, "Teaching Interactions.") Also, all Youth Care Workers learn how to promote positive relationships with each child. (See Chapter 8, "Relationship Building.")

Ongoing program evaluation

Regular evaluation reports provide administrators and direct care staff with systematic feedback on program effectiveness. These reports give all staff insight into the quality of care provided for children. One of the features of a humane program is how well it succeeds in reaching the goals for which it was established. Routine reporting of progress on important goals helps a program achieve its goals.

Regular youth interviews

Each child is interviewed when he or she leaves a shelter. During these interviews, each youngster is asked whether he or she was mistreated by Boys Town staff or others. Each child also is asked to express his or her opinion about the pleasantness and support of Youth Care Workers and others, and the overall effectiveness of the program. These questions provide important information regarding the atmosphere in the shelter. The emphasis here is on how goals are reached and what methods are used. Information derived from these questions can be used to improve staff interaction and communication skills, when necessary.

Feedback from outside consumers

Interested, involved persons from outside the shelter (teachers, probation officers, caseworkers, or family members) are another important source of information about the quality of care provided in Boys Town Shelters. These "consumers" are asked to assess the quality of care provided by each Youth Care Worker immediately following a youngster's departure. Outside consumers are an excellent source of impartial impressions of the care children receive.

Staff Practice Inquiries

Any questionable staff practice is followed up by a Staff Practice Inquiry. This inquiry is an investigation into a suspected inappropriate practice that stems from a youth report, a consumer report, or observation by staff.

All allegations concerning less-than-optimal care obtained from any source are investigated thoroughly and promptly. The fact that Staff Practice Inquiries are begun quickly makes it clear that Boys Town takes its protective role seriously. Boys Town investigates all claims, regardless of their perceived validity or their perceived seriousness. Even relatively benign allegations are investigated in order to sensitize all staff to the importance of maintaining high-quality standards of care.

It is the collective responsibility of all staff at Boys Town Shelters to safeguard the rights of children. Any suspected abuse observed by children, staff, or persons outside the shelter should be reported immediately to the Shelter Coordinator, Staff Supervisor, or Site Director. If such a report is received, administration immediately starts a Staff Practice Inquiry. The child and adult who were allegedly involved are interviewed along with others who may have relevant information. The facts are established and conclusions are reached as quickly as possible. Quick action is important so that a situation in which a child is in danger or is uncomfortable can be rectified. It's also important to act quickly so that any potential harm to a staff member's reputation can be minimized in situations where allegations are unfounded or untrue.

The greatest degree of confidentiality possible is maintained in all Staff Practice Inquiries. Total anonymity of the parties involved often can be maintained. Sometimes, however, anonymity cannot be guaranteed when a child may be at some risk. Relevant persons need some information during the course of the inquiry process. For instance, parents or legal guardians are immediately informed of any allegation. In cases where serious allegations are made, Child Protective Service agencies are informed so that they can decide whether or not to conduct their own investigation.

Another important phase of Staff Practice Inquiries is the debriefing phase. Verbal and/or written reports are given to persons who have the right to know about any outcomes. It is important that relevant persons are kept informed, not only to protect the interests of the child, but also to protect the reputation of any staff who are involved.

Training in the rights of children

All Boys Town staff who work with children receive Preservice Training to increase their sensitivity to the rights of children. Typically, this training occurs before staff begin to work with children. Subsequent to the Preservice Training, staff are updated through the consultant advisory process, and materials and meetings provided by administration. Staff are provided with specific rules about what to do or not to do in child-care situations, as well as less specific guidelines that augment the sound judgment required of any person involved in child care.

This chapter outlines and explains 14 specific youth rights. These are not all inclusive but give a good overview of the kinds of rights children have in Boys Town Shelters.

For each of these areas, there are both rules and guidelines. Rules are empirical generalizations, or "rules of thumb." Certain priorities are called "rules" because they are not to be modified. In the very rare circumstances when they might be modified, changes should never occur without advance permission from a Supervisor.

Guidelines, on the other hand, are less explicit generalizations than rules. They serve as guiding principles around which staff must exercise discretion and sound judgment, depending upon a youngster's needs and the circumstances faced by staff and the youngster. Guidelines are considered to be prudent practices in typical situations.

1. Right to nourishment

Staff must provide each child with healthy food and proper nutrition. A major right of each child is the right to healthy nourishment.

Rules:

- Staff must provide three nutritionally adequate meals to each youth each and every day.

- The three main meals (i.e., breakfast, lunch, and supper) should never be used as a consequence or sold as a privilege. A child has a right to these because he or she is a person.

- Meals should never be made intentionally less adequate, less tasty, or less nutritious for any reason.

- Medical advice and guardian consent should be obtained before initiating weight-loss programs.

Guidelines:

- Staff should provide a wide variety of nutritious foods for children, including ethnic preferences.

- Staff should avoid imposing their own personal food preferences on children (e.g., vegetarian or sugar-free diets) or fad diets (e.g., eggs and grapefruit for each meal).

- Nutritious snacks such as fruits or vegetables are best made freely available (e.g., apples after school).

- "Junk food" (e.g., chips, Big Macs, etc.) should be available only in moderation. Prohibiting "junk food," however, usually is unreasonable and unenforceable.

- Staff should be able to provide documentation of adequate nutrition (e.g., keep menus for six months).

2. Right to communicate with significant others

Staff should actively teach children how to communicate with others. Healthy relationships with significant others are desirable for all children.

Rules:

- Children have a right to seek advocacy or communicate with significant others like parents, guardians, probation officers, or clergy.

- Communication with significant others should not be used as a consequence or sold as a privilege (e.g., because Johnny did not apologize to his Youth Care Worker, he cannot call his mother).

- Staff should provide methods (i.e., mail or phone) for routine and emergency contact with significant others.

- Staff should advocate for each child's right to present his or her own case directly to any authority in any formal or informal proceedings.

Guidelines:

- Staff can exercise reasonable control over the form (e.g., two long-distance calls per week) and timing (e.g., allow a call to probation officer when child is calm) of communication.

- Control over the form, frequency, or timing of communication should not be unreasonable (e.g., even though a child is not calm, he or she can call a guardian after reasonable attempts have been made to calm the child; thus, after three hours of discussion, it would be prudent to let the child call).

3. Right to respect of body and person

Staff should use interaction styles that are the most pleasant and that demonstrate humane, professional, concerned care at all times. Physical interaction styles are strongly discouraged. Violence is always forbidden.

Rules:

- Corporal punishment is never used to discipline youngsters (e.g., never use spanking or physical exercise as a consequence).

- Staff should use restraint as a last option and only when it is necessary to prevent a child from harming himself or herself, or others.

- Staff should avoid sarcasm, labeling, or name-calling that might humiliate a child (e.g., discussing John's bed wetting at Daily Meeting).

- The use of curse words directed toward children is never appropriate.

Guidelines:

- It is best that outside agents such as police officers use restraint, when it is necessary. Restraint is most successful (i.e., prevents injury) when the adult has physical superiority and has been trained in restraint procedures.

- The least possible force should be employed when restraint is required.

4. Right to have one's own possessions

Each child has a right to possessions that are commensurate with their developmental level and their living situation. Staff should respect a youth's right to possessions and create a home atmosphere that facilitates children owning personal possessions.

Rules:

- Staff should ensure that children do not possess dangerous items (e.g., drugs, guns, knives).

- Staff should ensure that each child has the necessary possessions for school or job, and that possessions are similar to those of his or her peers (e.g., books, clothes, bedding, etc.).

- Staff should never confiscate a child's possessions (other than dangerous possessions) without having the child waive his or her right to the possession or without the intent to transfer physical custody of the possession to the child's guardian.

Guidelines:

- Children should come to a shelter with necessities (clothing, personal hygiene items, etc.) and should not be allowed to have portable stereos, TVs, weapons, etc. Staff can exercise reasonable control over the possessions a youngster brings to a shelter.

- Staff can limit the use of personal possessions to reasonable times or places (e.g., no playing ball indoors).

- If a child is restricted from appropriate use of a personal possession, he or she should be told how to earn its use back.

5. Right to privacy

Under the right to privacy, staff should ensure that each child has the rights typically afforded people in our society. Each child should have personal living and storage areas. Each child's right to physical privacy should be protected.

Rules:

- Staff should not open a child's mail or listen in on phone conversations without permission from the child.

- Staff shouldn't routinely or secretly search a child's room or belongings.

- Staff should not search a youngster's person.

- Staff can release program records only to a child's legal guardian or a person who has written permission from the child's legal guardian.

Guidelines:

- Staff should ensure privacy for each child and his or her belongings (e.g., bed, dresser, clothes) in the child's living space.

- Public searches (e.g., announced, with the child and one other adult present) for contraband may take place when there is probable cause to search.

- While staff should not open and read youth mail, a child can be asked to open mail in front of staff when there is probable cause (e.g., a child receiving drugs from a friend).

6. Right to freedom of movement

Each youth has a right to a wide range of experiences commensurate with his or her age and maturity level. Procedures that physically restrict movement or consequences that prevent exposure to healthy activities for extended periods of time are generally discouraged.

Rules:

- Staff should not use seclusion or "time-out" procedures as a discipline practice (e.g., locking a youth in a room or isolating a youth from the group).

- A child should always be provided with options for earning privileges (e.g., privileges can be earned on a Subsystem).

Guidelines:

- Staff can limit a youngster's movements to a given area and time (e.g., in school from 8 a.m. to 4:15 p.m., at the shelter from 4:30 p.m. to 6 p.m.).

7. Right to be given meaningful work

Staff should ensure that each youth lives in a learning environment where chores, tasks, goals, and privileges are meaningful experiences that enrich a child's body and mind. Ideally, consequences for problem behaviors should have an immediate teaching benefit and should not be principally punishing in nature.

Rules:

- Staff should never give "make work" tasks (e.g., cleaning a floor with a toothbrush, digging a hole and refilling it, or writing a sentence 500 times).

- Procedures that are designed solely to punish should not be employed (e.g., making a youth kneel and hold a broom above his or her head, or making a youth eat a catsup sandwich for squirting it on someone).

Guidelines:

- Staff can assign chores and tasks related to daily living that teach family or personal values (e.g., making one's bed or doing family dishes).

- Removing a youth from typical adolescent responsibilities (i.e., jobs, athletic teams, clubs, or choir) should not be a consequence for problem behaviors. Note: While a youth sometimes must be removed from these activities, this should be done only when the behavior is so serious that it negates the benefit of continued participation. The youth's participation can be resumed when the behavior improves.

8. Right to file material

Staff should make provisions for letting children know what is being communicated in Treatment Progress Reports. Written documentation should be consistent with daily treatment strategies and target areas. Good child care ensures that the child knows his or her treatment goals and progress.

Rules:

- Staff should not deny a child the right to know what they are writing in Treatment Progress Reports.

- A staff member should be present whenever a child is reviewing file material.

- Staff must ensure that all file material is secure and stored in a locked cabinet when they are not present to provide supervision.

Guidelines:

- Staff may routinely have youth sign Treatment Progress Reports.

- Sensitive file materials (e.g., psychological evaluation or social histories) should be stored in a locked file cabinet. This makes it less likely that a child will be exposed to confusing or emotionally laden material.

9. Right to interact with others

Youth should be taught skills that enhance their relationships with peers and adults. Youth should be provided with ample opportunities to interact with peers of the same and opposite sex. Interacting with people is a basic right. Staff should monitor each youngster's social contacts to ensure that they are appropriate.

Rules:

- Isolation should not be used as a consequence for problem behaviors (e.g., instructing other children not to talk to a child as a consequence for a problem behavior).

- Staff must provide children with appropriate opportunities to interact with the opposite sex. These interactions should always be well-monitored.

Guidelines:

- Staff may limit interactions between children and some peers (e.g., children with known substance abuse or sexual development problems may be limited in their interactions with peers with similar problems).

- Staff may limit when and how children interact with peers (e.g., limited out-of-shelter contacts on school nights or telephone-only contacts after 8 p.m. on school nights).

- Staff may ask other youth to leave the area when they are working with a particular youth, such as in an Intensive Teaching situation.

10. Right to goals and privileges

Commensurate with their age and development, each child should at all times have a Treatment Plan that provides the opportunity to work toward desired goals or privileges. All Motivation Systems should afford the youth an opportunity to earn some privileges. In addition to having a Treatment Plan, each child should know the specific behaviors that are needed to fulfill it.

Rules:

- No child should be given consequences that prohibit him or her from earning any privileges for unreasonably long periods of time (e.g., more than 24 hours).

- Children should have the opportunity to earn at least Basics, Snacks, TV, and one phone call every 24 hours.

- Children should not be given consequences without being told how they can remove the consequences and regain their privileges.

Guidelines:

- Staff should extend special advocacy for children who have not earned privileges for two days in succession (e.g., spend more time encouraging and interacting with a child).

11. Right to basic clothing necessities

Children should be provided with appropriate dress and leisure clothing commensurate with their age and sex. Staff should ensure that each child's basic clothing needs are met at all times.

Rules:

- Basic clothing needs should never be limited as a consequence for a problem behavior (e.g., child wears no coat as a consequence for losing it, or a child is forced to wear inadequate or inappropriate clothing as a consequence).

- Each child has a right to the same style, type, and quantity of clothing that is provided for other children.

Guidelines:

- A child's personal preference in clothing should be strongly considered by staff so long as the personal preference is not extremely deviant as regards to style or price (e.g., neither "punk" styles nor designer quality need to be provided).

- Staff can limit the style of clothing so that it is consistent with the treatment goals of an individual youth (e.g., a child should not wear sexually provocative clothing, or clothing that contains messages or material that is profane or related to drugs, alcohol, or cigarettes).

12. Right to the natural elements

Each child has a right to natural elements such as fresh air, light, sunshine, and outdoor exercise. Healthy outdoor activities should be a routine part of every child's experience. Staff should ensure that each child has the opportunity to experience the natural elements each day.

Rules:

- Neither the natural elements nor indoor light should be used as a consequence (e.g., a child should be able to get some outside exercise even when on a Subsystem).

Guidelines:

- Each child should be provided with the opportunity for outside activities each day (e.g., walking in the yard).

- Staff can regulate the amount of time spent outside and the degree of supervision provided for each child.

13. Right to one's own bed

Each youth has a right to a personal bed and a private sleeping area.

Rules:

- A child's access to a personal bed or bedding should never be restricted during normal sleeping hours.

Guidelines:

- Staff may have more than one youngster sharing a bedroom if ample space and privacy is provided.

- Staff may regulate a youngster's access to his or her bedroom during nonsleeping hours or limit privacy of the sleeping area when a child is at risk (e.g., when a child is suicidal).

14. Right to leave Boys Town Shelter

Staff must ensure that a child is provided care in accordance with the reasonable wishes of the legal guardian.

Children have the right to advocacy by their guardian. This includes the guardian's right to place or remove a child from a Boys Town Shelter.

Because their stay at a Boys Town Shelter is short-term, youth begin having visits from parents/legal guardians as soon as possible, provided, of course, that the visits are safe, legal, and in the best interests of the child and family.

Depending on a child's situation, it may be a good idea to "test the waters" by having the child visit home overnight before he or she actually goes home for good. That way, both the parents and the child know what areas need work and what areas have improved.

If John comes to the shelter on June 10, his parent contact sheet may look something like this:

6/10 John called his mother.

6/11 John called his mother. Conversation about school.

6/12 John called his mother and set up a visit.

6/14 Mrs. Jones came to shelter to visit John. Visit was positive.

6/15 John called mother. Talked about family.

6/17 Mrs. Jones came to take John on an outing. Positive.

6/20 Overnight visit. Positive visit, though Mrs. Jones reported John had a fight with a sister.

6/22 Youth Care Worker called mother and set up departure day.

Rules:

- Staff can not prohibit a child from returning home or going to another placement upon the request of his or her legal guardian.

Guidelines:

- Youth Care Workers may provide advocacy for a child staying at a Boys Town Shelter in the form of rationales and by acting promptly on a parent's or guardian's request to remove the child.

- Staff should not impede the orderly transition of a child from a Boys Town Shelter to his or her next placement.

▶ **Home visits and family reunification**

The youth at Boys Town Shelters often are victims of physical, sexual, and psychological abuse. Drugs and alcohol often play a large and destructive role in their lives and in the lives of their parents. Environmental factors also play a destructive, rather than constructive, role in the developmental lives of these children. Poverty, hunger, and despair are outcomes for some children. As a result of these factors, many boys and girls arrive at Boys Town Shelters with emotional problems. A sense of rejection, despair, and hopelessness pervades their lives. They have seen their parents, brothers, and sisters commit suicide to escape the terrible traumas of their lives. In many instances, these youngsters also have considered suicide as a way to resolve their problems. These young boys and girls have suffered substantial pain in their lives.

It is in the context of these statements that we must look at whether it is safe or unsafe, beneficial or harmful, for a youth to return to his or her home for a visit or to live permanently. As parents, we would not send our youngsters to live or play in an environment that we know is currently unsafe. As we review the process of home visits and family reunification for the youngsters at Boys Town Shelters, we must act as caring adults and be truthful enough to tell youth that they should not frequent a place that might be unsafe or harmful to them. We begin on the first day of admission to help both the youth and the parents discuss appropriate ways to create a safe and beneficial environment to which the youth can successfully return.

At the time of admission, an assessment of a youngster is completed. This assessment is reviewed by the shelter administration and by other staff members who determine what needs to be accomplished in terms of the youth's first Treatment Plan. As part of the Treatment Plan, the following set of criteria will help determine the possibility and extent of home visits and/or family reunification:

- What behaviors does the youth need to change before it will be safe or beneficial for the youth to visit or return home?

- What behaviors must the parents change or what must be changed in the home environment before it will be safe or beneficial for the youth to visit or return home?

- What interventions must the agency that placed the youth engage in to change parental behavior or the home environment so that going home will be safe and beneficial? How should the agency make this intervention known to the Boys Town Shelter and the youth's parents?

- What safeguards and procedures for monitoring home behaviors must be in place to ensure that a youth's visit or return home will be safe and beneficial?

These questions must be asked and answered by the youth, parents, and the agency members before the youth is officially admitted to a Boys Town Shelter. All parties are told that there must be improvement shown in all relevant areas before home visits or reunification can take place. These guidelines are explained and set at the beginning of each youth's stay and reviewed regularly so that there is no undue concern or surprise when a home visit is either approved or denied.

Boys Town Shelters take youngsters who cannot remain in their own homes because of personal, family, social, or environmental problems that jeopardize their ability to grow into a successful adult. If we take youngsters because of severe problems at home, then it is only logical that we do not return these youngsters to that same environment unless we can be assured that the chronic abuse and violence are no longer present. It is our obligation to make sure that all of our young people are never again abused or subjected to situations that could put them or others at risk.

▶ Summary

Boys Town Shelters are very concerned about protecting and ensuring the rights and privileges of their children. The guidelines and processes described in this chapter provide evidence of this concern. However, success in ensuring children's rights is not brought about by procedures alone; there also must be a "sense of quality" instilled in each staff person at a shelter. Each person understands that it is his or her competence in carrying out Treatment Plans and diligence in monitoring his or her own actions and the actions of others that makes the real difference. Rules, guidelines, and procedures are necessary, but it is the commitment to provide the highest quality care possible that ensures a safe environment for each child.

Problem-solving

Besides having skill deficits, children who enter Boys Town Shelters also bring with them a number of interpersonal, school, and family problems. And of course, as each youngster experiences the normal processes of adolescent development, he or she will encounter personal problems that require solutions.

As a Youth Care Worker, you are responsible for helping these youngsters resolve conflicts, plan for the future, and make decisions about how they will live their lives. To accomplish this goal, you must learn how to provide one-to-one problem-solving for the children in your care. This chapter focuses on the importance of this type of teaching, the steps to problem-solving, and behaviors you can use as you help to teach youth how to be more independent.

"Most people spend more time and energy going around problems than trying to solve them."

Henry Ford

▶ Teaching problem-solving

This kind of teaching is similar to traditional, academic teaching in that it emphasizes listening, empathy, and exploring feelings. You should not appear shocked by anything the youth say. It is very important for you to accept all kinds of feelings and to let each youngster know that it is okay to feel or think the way he or she does. This helps the youngster feel comfortable expressing his or her emotions, fears, and concerns about intimate or embarrassing events. It helps you to better understand the youth and put his or her current behavior in the context of those feelings.

At Boys Town Shelters, however, teaching goes beyond the traditional exploration of feelings and seeks to work out new, more appropriate responses to them. You must teach youth that while it is okay to feel or think a certain way, it is not okay to behave any way they want. Society holds all of us accountable for what we do.

Each part of the problem-solving method is important. At Boys Town Shelters, using the problem-solving steps provides an opportunity for the youth to explore their feelings, and helps them arrive at a specific plan of action to solve or deal with a problem situation.

Since many of the youngsters' problems develop as a result of their poor decision-making, problem-solving can help them learn to clearly think through an issue before making a decision. It also gives you the opportunity to guide the decision-making process. This method is easy for youth to understand and has proven to be more beneficial than traditional approaches.

Your goals during problem-solving sessions are to help the youth arrive at a viable solution to his or her problem and to teach the youth problem-solving skills. Because such teaching sessions also promote and establish trust between you and the youth, another important goal is to build relationships through expressions of concern, affection, respect, and interest in the youth's problems. As a youth confides in you and sees that such confidence is respected and is met with concern and helpfulness, he or she will feel more and more comfortable problem-solving with you.

Problem-solving is most appropriate when a youth needs to develop a plan to deal with a problem. The problem may be one that he or she is currently experiencing, or one the youth is anticipating. The problem may involve the youth's parents, siblings, teachers, friends, employer, girlfriend, boyfriend, or someone else. Such problems can range from how to talk with an employer who has treated the youth unfairly, to how to resist peer pressure, to deciding whether or not to participate in an activity.

The problem-solving process also can be used retrospectively. For example, you can review a past situation in which a youth did not make the best choice and have the youth "problem-solve" the situation again. In this way, if the same situation arises in the future, the youth will be better prepared to deal with it.

There are a number of situations when such problem-solving is not appropriate. These would include times when you are attempting to teach a youth a new skill. Preventive Teaching, not problem-solving, is the appropriate procedure here. You also should not problem-solve with a youth when dealing with inappropriate behaviors such as skill deficiencies, rule violations, or inattentive ongoing behavior. Those problem behaviors require the consistent, concerned use of Teaching Interactions.

At times, you may be tempted to problem-solve when a youth does not respond to your teaching attempts, especially when a youth is passive and withdrawn, or is complaining about unfairness. In such cases, it is important to stay on task, regain the youth's attention and cooperation, and complete the necessary teaching. Later, when the youth is calm and his or her behavior is appropriate, you may choose to begin a problem-solving session.

In situations where serious issues arise, you should seek professional guidance instead of trying to problem-solve with the youth alone. For example, you can help a youth work through a divorce or death in his or her family, but you need to recognize that those types of situations sometimes are so traumatic that professional counseling is necessary.

A final example is suicide ideation, which is so serious that it requires immediate contact with the administration.

In fact, anytime you feel uncomfortable with a situation, you should contact an administrator, who then will ask other qualified professionals to step in to help meet the child's needs.

In general, it often is beneficial for kids to go to someone outside the shelter to discuss issues that are bothering them. It is only natural that youth may feel more comfortable talking to someone other than you about some issues, even when those issues are not especially serious. This is because you control the point system and, therefore, control a youth's privileges. Sometimes, because youth are afraid they will lose points or privileges, they need outside people to confide in. You need to feel comfortable when youth turn to such outside resources, and help them locate resources that are appropriate.

▶ Problem-solving behaviors

Using supportive problem-solving behaviors can help you be more successful as you work with youth.

One of these behaviors involves maintaining an appropriate physical distance between you and a youth during a variety of verbal interactions. Being close to a youth can help him or her feel more comfortable during the process. Avoid sitting behind a desk or table, or having other physical barriers between you and the youth. Sitting next to a youth on a couch or in a chair directly across from him or her makes it easier for you to offer a pat on the back.

Using a variety of listening skills encourages youth to discuss issues and express themselves. You can show that you care about and respect what the youngster is saying by looking at him or her, not interrupting, frequently nodding, and, in general, being attentive.

Your verbal behavior during problem-solving sessions also can help make a youth feel comfortable and encourage involvement in the discussion. You can keep the youth on task and involved by offering verbal encouragement and praise (e.g., "It's really good that you're thinking this through."), and by asking clarifying questions and requesting more information (e.g., "Tell me a little more about what happened after that" or "Can you explain that a little more?").

Providing empathy during the discussion lets the youth know that you are trying to understand his or her feelings and point of view (e.g., "That must be very upsetting to you" or "Looks like you're really angry about that."). Empathy is very important in establishing rapport with a youth and encouraging him or her to discuss issues.

While all of these qualities are important to successful problem-solving, it also is important for you to include them in your day-to-day interactions with each child. You need to express care and concern, listen, offer empathy, etc., in everyday interactions, as well as during problem-solving. There should not be a dramatic change in your behavior when problem-solving with the youth. In Boys Town Shelters, nurturing, caring behavior occurs on a day-to-day basis. When you consistently express your concern and act in ways that demonstrate your commitment, youth are more likely to come to you with their problems.

▶ Problem-solving procedures

Boys Town Shelters use the **SODAS** method, a revision of a counseling process developed by Jan Roosa (1973), for problem-solving. This method allows you to guide the teaching and rational problem-solving process. **SODAS** is an acronym that stands for the following steps:

S Define the problem **situation**.

O Examine **options** available to deal with the problem.

D Determine the **disadvantages** of each option.

A Determine the **advantages** of each option.

S Decide on the **solution**.

This general framework has a great deal of utility and flexibility. The process can be used for individual and/or group problem-solving discussions, such as those that occur during Daily Meeting. Again, the supportive verbal and nonverbal behaviors discussed earlier will play an important role in every counseling session.

The following is an explanation of each of the **SODAS** components:

Situation

The problem-solving process begins with you helping the youth to clearly define the situation or problem. In some cases, the youth initially will present vague and emotional descriptions (e.g., "I'm sick of school" or "My folks don't care what happens to me."). You can use general clarifying questions or statements to help the youth more fully describe the issues (e.g., "Why don't you explain that some more."). However, it also may be necessary for you to ask direct, specific questions (e.g., "Why are you sick of school?" or "Did something happen during your visit?"). By calmly and skillfully asking specific questions, you can keep the youth involved and help the youth articulate a realistic description of the situation.

As you ask questions, provide empathy, concern, and encouragement to the youth. Without statements of empathy, concern, and encouragement, a series of specific questions becomes more like an interrogation that is apt to cause the youth to withdraw.

As the youth more clearly defines the situation, summarize what the youth is saying. (e.g., "You're saying that you're tired of getting picked on by a certain boy at school," or "What you would like is for your dad and mom to spend more time with you."). Such a summarization is particularly important before any options are discussed. It helps you to make certain that all relevant information has been reviewed and that you have an accurate picture of the youth's situation. If the summary is inaccurate or incomplete, the youth has the opportunity to correct any misperceptions. This is especially important at this point, since the remainder of the process is built around the defined situation. Without an accurate or clearly defined situation, it will be difficult to generate useful options and a viable solution.

Options

Asking the youth specific questions about how he or she might solve a problem or deal with a situation is the best way to help the youth generate options (e.g., "Can you think of a way to handle that?" or "What do you think you can do about this?"). After the youth suggests an option, you can continue to solicit additional options (e.g., "Can you think of any other ideas?").

Initially, the youth may have trouble thinking of an option or thinking of more than one option. Also, the option the youth suggests may not be very helpful or realistic. Whenever a youth is not able to offer an option, it is very important for you to remain nonjudgmental. Offer encouragement for the youth's participation (e.g., "Well good, you've come up with a second option. You're really trying to think this through.") or offer a neutral comment and a prompt for more

options (e.g., "Okay, that's one option. Can you think of another one?").

It may be difficult for you to remain nonjudgmental, especially when the youth suggests an option that would only result in more problems (e.g., "I'll just have to punch him out."). It is important for you to remember that your role at this point is only to get the youth to suggest options. When you get to the next step (examining the advantages and disadvantages of each option), you can help the youth judge the "wisdom" of the suggested options.

During the option phase, you may give your suggestions as well. However, this should be done only after the youngster has given all of his or her ideas. You may want to phrase the option as a question (e.g., "How about talking to the teacher after class?") so that the youth still feels involved in the process. Over time, youth will be better able to come up with options on their own, and will be more comfortable doing so.

Disadvantages and Advantages

After the youth has offered a number of options, you can help him or her think through the disadvantages and advantages of each one. Each option is examined in turn and the advantages and disadvantages are discussed. In a sense, you are trying to teach the youth that there is a cause-and-effect relationship between the child's decisions and what happens to him or her.

Again, your role is to skillfully guide the youth by asking general questions (e.g., "Can you think of any problems if you do that?" or "Are there any benefits for doing that?"). If the youth has difficulty thinking through the disadvantages and advantages, you can help by asking more specific questions (e.g., "Well, what do you think your teacher will do if you start a fight in his class?" or "Do you think she might be more willing to listen to you if you did that?").

There may be a number of advantages and disadvantages for any given option. Since the goal is to help the youth learn to think, it is important in this phase that you try to solicit as many as possible (e.g., "Can you think of any other advantages? Any other problems?"). Also, remain nonjudgmental and do not argue with the youth about his or her perceptions of the advantages and disadvantages. This can be difficult when the youth seems enthusiastic about the advantages of an option that may not be realistic or could result in a problem (e.g., "Yeah, it'd be great to fight it out because then he'd leave me alone and everybody would think I was bad."). Rather than argue about the advantage, you can simply acknowledge the child's view (e.g., "Okay, so you think that an advantage would be...."). Later, you can guide the youth's judgment during the discussion of the disadvantages (e.g., "What happens if you don't win? Could you get hurt? What will your teacher do if he hears you've fought with another student?").

If the youth clearly does not understand or cannot be prompted to offer an important advantage or disadvantage, offer your viewpoint and allow the youth to react.

After the disadvantages and advantages for the options have been discussed, summarize by reviewing each option and the associated advantages and disadvantages. This summary review further helps the youth understand the cause-and-effect relationships.

Solution

This phase involves having the youth select a solution and preparing him or her to successfully implement it.

As a result of examining advantages and disadvantages, the youth typically selects a workable option. It may not always be the best option, from your point of view, but it is important that it is the youth's option. The youth are more likely to try to make an option work if they are truly comfortable with it and feel that the choice is theirs.

After the youth has selected an option, you should encourage and reassure the youth that he or she can successfully implement the solution. To help the youth feel comfortable with his or her choice, answer any questions about how to successfully implement it.

Another way you can improve the youth's chance for success is to set up a role-play or practice session. These role-play sessions should be as realistic as possible. For example, if an employer is fairly abrupt and somewhat stern, you can best help the youth by portraying the employer in that manner. The role-play can be made more realistic if you respond to the youth in several possible ways. This will help the youth to be better prepared, more comfortable, and more likely to succeed.

While it is important to express confidence in the youth's ability to implement the solution, you should not promise that the solution will work. As the practice session ends, you should prompt the youth to check back after he or she has tried the solution. If the youth succeeds in solving the problem, you should praise the youth for doing so and for going through the problem-solving session. If the solution does not work, you need to be very supportive and empathetic. You and the youth can then return to the **SODAS** method to find another possible solution.

Learning to problem-solve is a complex task. Because participating in the process is so important, it is reasonable to award large positive point rewards for practicing. Also, because many youth have "solved" their problems in inappropriate ways in the past (e.g., running away, becoming aggressive), it is important to award positive points when a youth indicates he or she would like to talk about a problem (e.g., "I have a problem at school. Can you talk with me about it?").

To help youth complete the **SODAS** process, Youth Care Workers can use the Rationale Problem-Solving form (Figure 1, p. 153).

The use of the **SODAS** method is very important in teaching problem-solving skills to youth. However, there are many other types of formal and informal activities that make it easier to model and directly teach this problem-solving approach. Informally, there will be opportunities for discussions that may be prompted by television shows or world events. When youth express their opinions and points of view, it provides you with some ideal opportunities to get them to think about options, and to discuss the possible ramifications of their views and values. For

example, you and the youngsters may be riding in the shelter van and observe a young driver speed through an intersection, run a red light, and squeal his tires. At that point, one of the youth might comment about how he can hardly wait until he can have a car and be "bad." You could use this opportunity to ask the youth if they see any problems (disadvantages) with running red lights or speeding. You also could ask them for their ideas (options) about how to impress people with a car without engaging in unsafe or illegal activities. Such informal discussions can help youth learn to think ahead, to get their needs met in appropriate ways, and to understand how their actions can lead to possible consequences. All these behaviors are keys to thinking and problem-solving.

There will be more formal opportunities to use the **SODAS** method when a youth needs to develop a plan for the future. For instance, employment, school, going home, or deciding how to develop an area of interest all lend themselves to the **SODAS** process.

There also may be times when you will initiate a problem-solving session and use the **SODAS** process to help a youth develop a plan for more personal issues (e.g., making friends, personal hygiene, etc.). It is important that you take a proactive approach to such sessions as well as being receptive to sessions initiated by a youth.

▶ Summary

In summary, problem-solving has two important goals – to help youth solve their problems and to teach youth how to solve problems in a systematic, rational way. The

SODAS method, combined with important quality components (i.e., empathy, listening skills, etc.) discussed in this chapter, can help you accomplish both goals.

"Sometimes the best way to forget your own problems is to help someone else solve theirs."

Hal Boyle

Figure 1

Boys Town Emergency Shelter Services
Rational Problem-Solving
The SODAS Method

Name: _____

S: _____

O: 1. _____
    2. _____
    3. _____

D: 1. a. _____   2. a. _____
      b. _____   b. _____
      c. _____   c. _____

                 3. a. _____
                      b. _____
                      c. _____

A: 1. a. _____   2. a. _____
      b. _____   b. _____
      c. _____   c. _____

                 3. a. _____
                      b. _____
                      c. _____

S: _____

SKILLS TO USE: _____

_____

CHAPTER TWENTY

Daily meeting and reporting problems

When youngsters are given a voice in decisions that affect their lives, they can begin to feel that what they think and have to say is important. This is a big step toward teaching youth how to control their behaviors and how to make good choices. At Boys Town Shelters, boys and girls have the opportunity to actively participate in this decision-making process through the Daily Meeting.

The Daily Meeting is a meeting of all the youth and Youth Care Workers that occurs everyday, usually in the evening. It also may occur at any other time during the day if a concern arises. (Meetings can be held more than once a day.) Sometimes, meetings are helpful just before the group leaves the shelter for an outing so that the youth know what behaviors are expected. Daily Meetings should last 10 to 20 minutes.

There are two types of Daily Meeting. The most common is one organized and conducted by the staff ; this is called a Staff Daily Meeting. The second type is the Youth Daily Meeting, which is organized and conducted by the youth.

This chapter will discuss the purposes and details of Daily Meetings, as well as how they are conducted.

▶ Daily Meeting goals

The first goal of Daily Meetings is to teach rational problem-solving skills. This involves the **SODAS** method (Chapter 19), and is an effective way to teach youth to consider the specific positive and negative outcomes of a situation before arriving at a rational conclusion.

A second goal of Daily Meetings is to share information. There are times when everyone at the shelter needs to know about an upcoming event, a change in rules, etc. For example, you may have a guest coming to the shelter and want to let the youth know about the visitor. Or, the bedtime for the youth may need to be changed, and this change needs to be announced to all youth. Many circumstances and situations can be communicated more efficiently in a group setting, and the Daily Meeting is the tool used to accomplish this.

Daily Meetings also provide an excellent opportunity for teaching morality and values. Youth Care Workers can offer their views on issues that are discussed and tell the youth how they would handle certain situations. In this way, Youth Care Workers act as role models for the youth as they share their morality and values. This is very important in reinforcing the positive behaviors and rationales that youth are learning.

A Daily Meeting also is another time when relationships are built and strengthened. Meetings allow for interactions in a different setting, outside the normal routine of the shelter. Staff behavior during meetings plays an essential role in relationship-building. For example, if a youth is trying to make a serious point and the other youth laugh at her, Youth Care Workers can show sensitivity by telling the youth that what she has to say is important, and asking the other youth to listen and remain quiet. This strengthens the bond between that youth and the staff, and sets a good example for the other youth.

Teaching the curriculum skills that were discussed in Chapter 4 is yet another

goal of Daily Meetings. This is accomplished in two ways. First, skills are taught through the behaviors that are expected and addressed. Second, skills are taught through group role-playing or group discussions about the skills, their components, and how they are used.

Finally, Daily Meetings serve as an excellent setting for teaching self-government. The youth at Boys Town Shelters have an opportunity to make real decisions based on rational discussion and voting. They can use the meeting as a mechanism for appropriately disagreeing with shelter rules or consequences, and for discussing issues that interest or bother them. Here, they're able to participate in a system where they have some control, and can help make decisions and set goals that can have a positive effect on everyone in the program.

▶ Skills to teach

A Daily Meeting is a wonderful time to teach skills and should be used to its greatest potential. As mentioned earlier, there are two ways to teach curriculum skills during Daily Meetings: 1) telling the youth what skills they will be expected to use during the meeting, and 2) role-playing or discussing a particular skill as a topic of the meeting.

Stating skill expectations is a teaching method that should be used consistently. This makes it more likely that the youth will respond to the staff's teaching, and will start using the skills in the shelter. Some of the skills that should be taught and reinforced through consequences during Daily Meetings include conversation skills, listening skills, giving criticism, accepting criticism, participating, reporting problems, and showing sensitivity to others. The components of these skills are found in the Boys Town manual, *Teaching Social Skills to Youth*.

Role-playing and discussing social skills as a meeting topic is a good way to teach a large number and variety of skills. Youth Care Workers can teach skills that are of a particular concern to the youth (i.e., peer relations, accepting criticism), or can address new skills. When teaching the youth using either of these two methods, Youth Care Workers should use Preventive Teaching or Planned Teaching ahead of time.

▶ Rationales for Daily Meeting

We have touched on several goals of Daily Meeting. Let's look at the two most important reasons for having them.

First, Daily Meetings teach the youth how to get along in group settings. Some youth have difficulty in school or other situations where they must deal with groups of people. Daily Meetings provide added direction and practice in working and getting along with others.

Second, Daily Meetings can be used to get the shelter "back on track." There will be times in the shelter when things seem to be a little chaotic; when this happens, everyone needs to get together to talk over the situation. Daily Meetings allow the staff to get the youth to sit down, decide what needs done, and communicate their decisions. These are valuable discussions, and should be used as needed.

▶ Youth Care Worker behavior

Before each Daily Meeting, Youth Care Workers decide which one of them will lead the meeting. That person acts as the discussion leader while the other workers participate in the discussions and monitor the behavior of the youth.

The Youth Care Workers also use Effective Praise to reinforce appropriate youth behavior during the meeting, keeping in mind each youth's individual treatment goals. Praise should be given for behaviors like contributing to discussions and making suggestions, using good rationales, staying on task, and using newly learned behaviors or target skills. Youth Care Workers also use prompts and cues to help the youth remember appropriate behavior, without interrupting the flow of the discussion. Furthermore, they teach the concepts of pleasantness, effectiveness, fairness, and concern by pairing those words with specific behaviors that relate to those concepts. This helps the youth learn the meaning of the concepts and their importance in everyday life.

For inappropriate behavior, Youth Care Workers should use Teaching Interactions and give consequences, just as they would if those behaviors occurred outside the Daily Meeting. This is an effective way to teach youth, especially when an interaction includes a positive correction statement (e.g., "If you can continue this discussion without any more yelling or interrupting, you can earn back half the points you just lost."). If Teaching Interactions don't work and a youth's inappropriate behavior continues to escalate, the Youth Care Workers should stop the meeting, deal with the problem, and resume the meeting later.

Finally, the Youth Care Workers guide the Daily Meeting and keep the discussion focused on the topics, prompt the use of rationales, and offer summaries before votes are taken to make sure that the youth understand the issues and all the options that are available. In the final analysis, you and your fellow Youth Care Workers are responsible for all decisions made in a shelter, including those made at a Daily Meeting. If the youth approve consequences or rules that are unfair or abusive, or decide to discuss issues that are inappropriate or personal, the Youth Care Workers must redirect the decision or discussion in order to ensure fair treatment for everyone.

As we mentioned earlier, there are two types of Daily Meeting. The next sections will discuss each one in more detail.

▶ Staff Daily Meetings

In a Staff Daily Meeting, Youth Care Workers organize and conduct the meeting, and decide on topics or information that will be discussed or presented. These meetings usually focus on problem-solving, goal-setting, curriculum skills, and program education. Occasionally, a game or activity can be planned.

Staff Daily Meetings usually take place once a day, or as needed if a concern arises. If an issue or situation that requires immediate attention comes up, a Daily Meeting should be held so that the staff and youth can work through the situation. "As needed" Daily Meetings also are good times to make special announcements or review skills before outings.

▶ Youth Daily Meetings

Youth Daily Meetings are organized and conducted by the shelter youth. However, Youth Care Workers should use caution when deciding whether to have this type of meeting. They should feel comfortable with their own abilities to conduct orderly and effective Staff Daily Meetings, and be confident that the youth can take on the responsibilities of organizing and conducting a meeting. Youth Daily Meetings require extra effort and skilled staff.

The main reason for having Youth Daily Meetings is to give the youth more ownership in the Daily Meeting process and to increase participation. The youth are responsible for choosing a discussion topic (through voting), selecting a presenter (usually a volunteer), and making all other preparations. One key element to the meeting is tying a curriculum skill to the topic. So if the discussion topic is illegal drugs, the youth might choose to talk about the curriculum skill of "Resisting Peer Pressure."

Youth Care Workers can make comments during the meetings, but most of the discussion should come from the youth. However, Youth Care Workers should address negative behavior and redirect questionable discussions without hesitation.

Figure 1 and Figure 2 are two forms that are designed to help youth organize their meetings. Figure 1 is a list of possible discussion topics. Figure 2 is a set of guidelines for preparing for a meeting and presenting information during a meeting.

Figure 1

Youth Daily Meeting Topics

Abandoned people	Driving
Homeless people	Rules – family, society
Abortion	Drug abuse
Jobs	Runaways
Academics	Euthanasia
Money	Self-discipline
AIDS	Emotional abuse
Music	Sports
Blended families	Families
Pets/Animals	Teen pregnancy
Clothing	Friendships
Physical abuse	TV shows
Crime	Gangs
Poverty	Unemployment
Current events	Goal-setting
Racism	Verbal abuse
Date rape	Gun control
Role models	Voting
	Hobbies

Figure 2

Youth Daily Meeting Worksheet

1. What topics were suggested?

2. Which topic are you most interested in? Which topic could you present better?

3. Research your topic.

4. Write down 10 questions you could ask about the topic.

5. Are there any tools that you could use to make the presentation more interesting (i.e., easel, newspaper, a questionnaire, current event)?

6. What skills from the manual, *Teaching Social Skills to Youth*, could be used with this topic?

7. Find one skill that you will teach and write out all the steps.

8. Practice what you have prepared.

9. Role-play your Daily Meeting topic with a Youth Care Worker or another youth.

The Presentation

1. Speak in a clear voice tone.

2. Maintain eye contact with all youth.

3. Stay on task.

4. Prompt other youngsters' behavior if necessary.

5. Direct questions to all youth.

6. Be prepared to answer questions from the youth.

7. REMEMBER – YOU are in charge of the meeting.

8. Begin closure of the topic/skill after approximately 15 minutes.

▶ Reporting problems

A Daily Meeting also is an excellent time to teach youth the importance of reporting problems that might affect someone in the shelter. (This is also known as peer reporting.) As a Youth Care Worker, you must teach the youth that the shelter has each resident's best interests at heart. This includes looking out for each person in the shelter and helping to identify and solve problems.

Helping each other should be everyone's goal at a shelter. "Everyone" does not just refer to Youth Care Workers, teachers, therapists, and other adults; "everyone" also means the youth. That means that each youngster is expected to report his or her own problems and the problems of his or her peers at the shelter.

This is a big responsibility for the youth. But they must learn that reporting problems is a way of showing concern for themselves and others. It shows that they care enough to point out problems and to enlist the help of the Youth Care Workers and other youth to solve them. Reporting problems also is a form of self-discipline and self-guidance.

Obviously, the idea behind reporting problems is to help the youth stay out of trouble. The Youth Care Workers cannot be everywhere at once, so a good reporting system helps them monitor the behavior of all youth each day.

Because it is so important for youth to learn to take responsibility for what happens in the shelter, the concept needs to be introduced to a youngster shortly after he or she comes to the shelter. To encourage youth to take on this responsibility, Youth Care

Workers should give them a lot of points for showing their concern in this way. The youngsters must understand that if they do not report inappropriate behaviors, it shows a lack of concern and makes them accomplices to the misbehavior. So, if Jim did something inappropriate, and Frank and John saw it but did not report it, Frank and John also would lose points. (Jim's point loss would be larger than those of the two boys since his inappropriate behavior is more serious than Frank and John not reporting it.)

There are three levels of point fines based on the reporting system:

1. Self-report – If a youth does something wrong and then promptly reports the behavior to a Youth Care Worker, he or she receives a regular point fine (based on the seriousness of the behavior). However, the youth would earn back points for making a self-report.

2. Peer report – If a youth does something wrong and another youth reports it to a Youth Care Worker, the first youth receives a larger-than-normal point fine and the youth who reported the incident receives a point reward. However, Youth Care Workers need to make sure that youth don't turn peer reporting into tattling, just to earn points.

3. Public report – If a youth does something wrong and someone outside the shelter (i.e., neighbor, teacher, police officer, etc.) reports it to the Youth Care Workers, the youth receives a larger-than-normal point fine for the misbehavior and an additional point fine for the public report of the misbehavior. In this case, if other youth knew about the incident and did not report it, they would receive a similar point fine for the pubic report.

Thus, self-reports result in the smallest point fines while public reports always result in a more substantial point fine. If a youth actively discourages a peer from engaging in an inappropriate behavior, that youth would earn a lot of points and praise from the Youth Care Workers for showing his or her concern for others in the group.

▶ Summary

Daily Meetings provide an opportunity to discuss problems, achievements, and other issues that affect youth while they are in a shelter. Effectively teaching youth the appropriate behaviors for such meetings is a key to having successful discussions.

These meetings also are a great way to communicate. They allow information, skills, values, morals, etc., to be shared in a positive, fun, efficient way. The meetings are a valuable tool and should be used in the shelter setting by skilled Youth Care Workers who understand the Daily Meeting process.

Reporting problems is another responsibility the youth must assume during their shelter stay. Youth are expected to report their own misbehaviors or problems as well as those of other youth. This concept helps youth learn how to show concern for others. Points are awarded when youth report misbehaviors, and youth receive point fines for failing to share such information with Youth Care Workers.

References

Bedlington, M.M., Braukmann, C.J., Raup, K.A., & Wolf, M.M. (1988). A comparison of treatment environments in community-based group homes for adolescent offenders. Special issue: Community psychology perspectives on delinquency. **Criminal Justice and Behavior, 15**(3), 349-363.

Braukmann, P.D., Ramp, K.K., Braukmann, C.J., Willner, A.G., & Wolf, M.M. (1983). The analysis and training of rationales for child care workers. **Children and Youth Services Review, 5**, 177-194.

Eitzen, D.S. (1974). Impact of behavior modification techniques on locus of control of delinquent boys. **Psychological Reports, 35(3)**, 1317-1318.

Elder, G.H. Jr. (1963). Parental power legitimation and its effect on the adolescent. **Sociometry, 26**, 50-65.

Roosa, J.B. (1973). **SOCS: Situations, options, consequences, simulation: A technique for teaching social interactions**. Unpublished paper presented to the American Psychological Association, Montreal.

Willner, A.G., Braukmann, C.J., Kirigin, K.A., Fixsen, D.L., Phillips, E.L., & Wolf, M. (1977). The training and validation of youth-preferred social behaviors of child-care personnel. **Journal of Social Work, 10**, 219-230.

Bibliography

Ackerson, L. (1931). **Children's behavior problems** (Vol. 1). Chicago: University of Chicago Press.

Bandura, A. (1969). **Principles of behavior modification**. New York: Holt, Rinehart, and Winston.

Behar, D., & Stewart, M.A. (1982). Aggressive conduct disorder of children. **Acta Psychiatric Scandinavia, 65**, 210-220.

Dishion, T.J., Loeber, R., Stouthamer-Loeber, M., & Patterson, G.R. (1984). Skill deficits and male adolescent delinquency. **Journal of Abnormal Child Psychology, 12**, 37-54.

Edelbrock, C. (1983). **The antecedents of antisocial behavior: A cross-sectional analysis**. Unpublished manuscript, University of Pittsburgh School of Medicine.

Farrington, D.P. (1978). The family background of aggressive youths. In L.A. Hersov, M. Berger, & D. Schaffer (Eds.), **Aggressive and antisocial behavior in childhood and adolescence** (pp. 73-94). Oxford, England: Pergamon Press.

Gilbert, G.M. (1957). A survey of "referral problems" in metropolitan child guidance centers. **Journal of Clinical Psychology, 13**, 37-42.

Gittelman, M. (1965). Behavior rehearsal as a technique in child treatment. **Journal of Child Psychology and Psychiatry, 6**, 251-255.

Glueck, S., & Glueck, E.T. (1950). **Unravelling juvenile delinquency**. Cambridge, MA: Harvard University Press.

Glueck, S., & Glueck, E.T. (1968). **Delinquents and nondelinquents in perspective**. Cambridge, MA: Harvard University Press.

Hetherington, E.M., & Martin, B. (1979). In H.C. Quay & J.S. Werry (Eds.), **Psychopathological disorders of childhood** (2nd ed.). New York: Wiley.

Hirschi, T., & Hindeland, M.J. (1977). Intelligence and delinquency: A revisionist review. **American Sociological Review, 42**, 571-587.

Kazdin, A.E. (1985). **Treatment of antisocial behavior in children and adolescents**. Homewood, IL: The Dorsey Press.

Ledingham, J.E., & Schwartzman, A.E. (1984). A 3-year follow-up of aggressive and withdrawn behavior in childhood: Preliminary findings. **Journal of Abnormal Child Psychology, 12**, 157-168.

Lesser, G.S. (1959). The relationships between various forms of aggression and popularity among lower-class children. **Journal of Educational Psychology, 50**, 20-25.

MacFarlane, J.W., Allen, L., & Honzik, M.P. (1954). **A developmental study of the behavior problems of normal children 21 months and 14 years**. Berkeley: University of California Press.

McCord, W., McCord, J., & Zola, J.K. (1959). **Origins of crime**. New York: Columbia University Press.

Nye, F.I. (1958). **Family relationships and delinquent behavior**. New York: John Wiley & Sons.

Patterson, G.R. (1982). **Coercive family process**. Eugene, OR: Castalia.

Patterson, G.R., DeBaryshe, B.D., & Ramsey, E. (1989). A developmental perspective on antisocial behavior. **American Psychologist,** February, 329-335.

Patterson, G.R., Dishion, T.J., & Bank, L. (1984). Family interaction: A process model of deviancy training. **Aggressive Behavior, 10**, 253-267.

Patterson, G.R., Dishion, T.J., & Reid, J.B. (1992). **A social learning approach: Volume 4, a coercion model**. Eugene, OR: Castalia.

Patterson, G.R., & Forgatch, M. (1987). **Part 1: The basis, parents and adolescents living together**. Eugene, OR: Castalia.

Patterson, G.R., & Stouthamer-Loeber, M. (1984). The correlation of family management practices and delinquency. **Child Development, 55**, 1299-1307.

Phillips, E.L., Phillips, E.A., Fixsen, D., & Wolf, M.M. (1974). **The teaching-family handbook**. Lawrence, KS: University Printing Service.

Pikas, A. (1961). Children's attitudes toward rational versus inhibiting parental authority. **Journal of Abnormal Social Psychology, 62**, 313-321.

Robins, L.N. (1966). **Deviant children grown up**. Baltimore: Williams & Wilkins.

Robins, L.N. (1978). Sturdy childhood predictors of adult antisocial behavior: Replications from longitudinal studies. **Psychological Medicine, 8**, 611-622.

Rutter, M., & Giller, H. (1983). **Juvenile delinquency: Trends and perspectives**. New York: Penguin Books.

Rutter, M., Tizard, J., & Whitmore, K. (Eds.). (1970). **Education, health and behavior**. London: Longmans.

Snyder, J., Dishion, T.J., & Patterson, G.R. (1986). Determinants and consequences of associating with deviant peers during preadolescence and adolescence. **Journal of Early Adolescence, 6**, 29-43.

Sturge, C. (1982). Reading retardation and antisocial behavior. **Journal of Child Psychology and Psychiatry, 23**, 21-31.

Wadsworth, M. (1979). **Roots of delinquency: Infancy, adolescence and crime**. New York: Barnes & Noble.

Werry, J.S., & Quay, H.C. (1971). The prevalence of behavior symptoms in younger elementary school children. **American Journal of Orthopsychiatry, 41**, 136-143.

West, D.J. (1982). **Delinquency: Its roots, careers and prospects**. Cambridge, MA: Harvard University Press.

Wolfgang, M.E., Figlio, R., & Sellin, T. (1972). **Delinquency in a birth cohort**. Chicago: University of Chicago Press.

█ndex